Outcries and Asides

BOOKS BY J. B. PRIESTLEY INCLUDE

FICTION

Adam in Moonshine
Benighted
The Good Companions
Angel Pavement
Faraway
Wonder Hero
Laburnum Grove
They Walk in the City
The Doomsday Men
Let the People Sing
Blackout in Gretley
Daylight on Saturday
Three Men in New Suits
Bright Day

Jenny Villiers
Festival at Farbridge
The Other Place: short stories
The Magicians
Low Notes on a High Level
Saturn Over the Water
The Thirty-First of June
The Shapes of Sleep
Sir Michael and Sir George
Lost Empires
It's an Old Country
Out of Town (The Image Men—I)
London End (The Image Men—II)
Snoggle

COLLECTED PLAYS

Volume I
Dangerous Corner
Eden End
Time and the Conways
I Have Been Here Before
Johnson over Jordan
Music at Night
The Linden Tree

Volume II
Laburnum Grove
Bees on the Boat Deck
When we are Married
Good Night Children
The Golden Fleece
How are they at Home?
Ever Since Paradise

Volume III
Cornelius
People at Sea
They Came to a City
Desert Highway
An Inspector Calls
Home is Tomorrow
Summer Day's Dream

ESSAYS AND AUTOBIOGRAPHY

Midnight on the Desert
Rain upon Godshill
Delight
All About Ourselves and other Essays
  (chosen by Eric Gillett)

Thoughts in the Wilderness
Margin Released
The Moments and other pieces
Essays of Five Decades
Over the Long High Wall

CRITICISM AND MISCELLANEOUS

The English Comic Characters
English Journey
Journey Down a Rainbow
  (with Jacquetta Hawkes)
The Art of the Dramatist
Literature and Western Man
The World of J. B. Priestley
  (edited by Donald G. MacRae)

Trumpets over the Sea
The Prince of Pleasure and
  his Regency
The Edwardians
Victoria's Heyday
The English
A Visit to New Zealand

J. B. PRIESTLEY

Outcries and Asides

HEINEMANN: LONDON

William Heinemann Ltd
15 Queen Street, Mayfair, London W1X 8BE

LONDON MELBOURNE TORONTO
JOHANNESBURG AUCKLAND

First published 1974
© J. B. Priestley 1974
SBN: 434 60361 9

Printed in Great Britain
by W & J Mackay Limited, Chatham

For Jacquetta and the family
with enduring love—and in the hope
they have not already had
too much of this sort of thing

Contents

Preface

IN AN EARLIER period a book of this kind would almost
certainly have been entitled *Table Talk*. This does not seem
to me to rule out my choice of *Outcries and Asides*, if only
because good talk, varying in intimacy, includes both of
these. On the other hand, after giving the question some
thought, I decided against dividing the book in terms of
either subject matter or mood, preferring to present its
pieces in exactly the order in which they were written—at
odd intervals during the last few years. A few of them, now
abridged, were taken from a feature, known as *The Uneasy
Chair*, that ran for some time in *The New Statesman*, and I
thank the present Editor for permission to include this
material here. Finally, I make no apology for writing so
much about myself in this volume. A liberal allowance of
egotism has always been demanded by any honest author
of Table Talk, even though I think my friends would agree
that in actual talk I am rarely inclined to go on and on
about myself. And after all it is easy enough to turn a few
pages and discover a fairly rich variety of topics.

J.B.P.

Music

COMING BACK FROM my afternoon walk, lying full-
length on the study couch, then listening to some fine
recordings, what follows has often haunted me. I cannot
escape the feeling that music of any quality, though made
by man, is too good for us. It suggests far superior beings.
Its joys and sorrows, its despair and hope, belong to existences larger than ours, more sensitive yet more enduring.
It escapes from our persistent littleness, our dwarfish
mean squabbling, our mobs of half-blind midgets. Its drama
is about something else going on somewhere else: we are
really peeping and eavesdropping. I am always astonished
that musicians should have any respect for writers, for I
always feel that they have just returned from—or are about
to go to—regions that would never offer me a foothold and
have immeasurable chasms and peaks of glory, clear to
their eyes and only a remote dazzle to mine. No doubt they
have agents, press cuttings, arguments about billings and
percentages, but these, I feel, are little games they play, to
meet us easily on our level. But their art rises far above it,
does not report our affairs but gives us glimpses of giants,
mighty sorcerers and magicians, battles between demons
and angels, immortal lovers wandering across the fields of
Paradise.

Irish and English

RE-READING YEATS' *On The Boiler* I find much of it
affected and false and some of it plainly detestable. But I
like this:

> My best-informed relative says: 'Because Ireland is a
> backward country everybody is unique and knows that
> if he tumbles down somebody will pick him up. But an
> Englishman must be terrified, for there is a man exactly
> like him at every street corner.'

Yeats himself would have been a great poet anywhere, I
feel, but I also feel that many lesser Irish writers enjoyed
reputations they might never have won if they had been
English. Moreover—and this is rarely acknowledged—so
many Irish writers, Yeats included, were greatly in debt to
one London publishing house, Macmillan, and to a loyal
and enthusiastic body of English, not Irish, readers, of
whom, from my middle teens, I was one.

Characters in Fiction

IT IS NOW many many years since there came a reaction
against the elaborate descriptions of characters found in
Victorian novels. Most of us, if we knew our job, contented
ourselves with a fairly brief account of our characters'

appearances, just about what you would take in when you first met them. But now, in one new novel after another, all too often nobody is described at all. This fascinating girl who—God knows why!—keeps taking the anti-hero to bed —what does she look like?—is she tall, medium, short, plump, thin, fair, mousy, dark, long-nosed, snub-nosed, thick-lipped, thin-lipped, fat-cheeked, hollow-cheeked, what what, what? We don't know. We aren't given a clue. Perhaps the novelist hasn't one himself. We know what anti-hero looks like, because in the first chapter he stares at himself before shaving and of course cutting himself. But then we are tired of him. It would be all the same to most of us if he didn't cut his chin but his throat.

Advertisement

SOMEBODY MUST ANSWER that advertisement, so I am doing it. *The Rylands are always on the go—are you?* No, I am not—and just keep your Rylands well away from me.

Our Address

DURING THE YEARS we have lived here, at Kissing Tree House, Alveston, I have had to give it as my address innumerable times. Men stare or frown, as if they did not hear me properly. But the women, of all ages, cry, 'Oh— what a lovely name!'

Ideologies

IN MEDIEVAL NUREMBERG, you may remember, some wretched prisoners were condemned to torture or final execution by the Iron Virgin or Maiden. They were placed inside this hollow effigy, which had a number of spikes that began to inflict terrible wounds and would finally kill them when it was completely closed. The Iron Maidens of our age are the ideologies, whether of the Left or the Right. Ordinary humanity is forced inside them, and then begins to bleed. People have to conform to the idea. It is not designed to suit them. The ideologies are just about as flexible and accommodating as the Iron Maiden and its spikes. So men who in their youth decided to serve man-kind and then accepted an ideology, one or other world-saver, will in middle age be found condoning starvation, torture and murder. Such men need not be Communists or Fascists, they may be ideological advocates of capitalist free enterprise and what they call democracy. These servants of the master plan, the world-saving idea, nearly always dislike ordinary people, so vaguely untidy in their notions, so inconsistent, so narrow in their outlook, so maddening in their suspicion of the ideology, that they deserve to be punished and to suffer. One depressing feature of the shouting in the colleges and the streets is that so many of the protesters seem to want to destroy one ideology only to put in its place another, even more rigid. Academics, pedants, bureaucrats, who want everything cut-and-dried, all neatly planned, nearly always favour ideologies, and sneer at vague reformers, the hopeful woolly-minded, those who want to move in a certain direction and not force everybody into an exact plan, and all the bumbling people who don't know exactly what they do want but do know what they don't want. Among these the majority are women, who shrink from the dogmatism, rigidity, and underlying inhumanity of an ideology. On the other hand, those women who are slaves to an ideology are horrors, Iron Maidens with the sharpest spikes.

Don't Do It

WHEN YOU ARE very widely-known as a writer—as I used to be but am no longer now—you are cajoled, persuaded, pressed to do a lot of things you don't want to do. You sign petitions, join deputations, address meetings, talk on radio and appear on television, when you would rather be working or idling at home. This is bad enough but it is even worse when writers who have refused to do things they didn't want to do, who have steadily remained working or idling at home, not putting themselves out for anybody, are praised for their dedication, their integrity, their professional purity—and often by the very people who insisted upon dragging you away from your fireside to make a public show of yourself. So—advice to a young writer: don't do a dam' thing for anybody.

Character Part

WHAT FOLLOWS MAY have been said before—and said better—but I am too lazy to find out: so here goes. As we reach old age we find ourselves mysteriously compelled to play a character part. However, we need not identify ourselves with it. I don't. So, to my surprise, I hear myself making those odd noises—loud hums and ha's and throat-clearings—that I used to find so irritating in old people. I catch myself moving more slowly and heavily than I need to do. At any time now, I feel, the character part will make me begin a patronising and intolerable speech with 'My dear boy, when you're my age you'll realise—'. Yet inside, behind all this histrionic rubbish, I shall be little different from what I have been for the last sixty years.

Time Wasters

AT ONE END of my desk, as I write this, there is a transcript of a taped interview with me, sent by an American university. It is very long; there are many words that ought not to be there; and a number of blanks I am asked to fill. I could find myself wasting a couple of hours trying to put the thing right. Last week I returned to another American university, one I have never set eyes on, a huge questionnaire that might easily use up half a day. I don't know what other men do, but, returning this time-wasting monster, I said quite truthfully that I had made a rule never to attend to questionnaires. The people who devise these things and send them out are pests—and enough is enough.

Mushroom Magic

IT IS ONLY in September that I regret having left the Isle of Wight for these Midlands. Oh—those hazy–golden September afternoons when we wandered over the high Down opposite our house—picking mushrooms! It was as if we were restored to the enchantments of childhood. Picking mushrooms has everything to content the heart and uplift the spirit. (But of course you must enjoy, as I do, eating large fresh mushrooms, not those miserable little objects grown in deep cellars.) Let us consider briefly what this glorious mushroom-gathering offers us. First then, all the ancient joys of Hunting and Searching and Treasure-seeking. Next—and I can't pretend this doesn't matter Something for Nothing and, as yet, off-tax. Finally, and best of all, *Magic*! The mushroom itself is magical, refusing all

[7]

vegetable routines, coming up when and where it pleases, here today without a sign of it yesterday, for ever mixing disappointment with triumph, as if it belonged to some underground kingdom of gnomes, half-mocking half-kindly, mean on Tuesday, generous on Wednesday. This magical element, for which the mushroom has been re-nowned throughout the ages, entangles us, the pickers, in its sorcery, so that stout middle-aged authors and their wives begin rushing here and there, laughing aloud. For once outside our steel and concrete and carbon monoxide civilisation, we spend the afternoon doing what our remote ancestors must have done, with equal enjoyment and racial memories stir our depths. Next year we must go back to the Island, just in time for the mushrooms. But of course, being mushrooms and never allowing themselves to be taken for granted, they may not be there. And equally of course the gold of those afternoons may have faded, and we may find ourselves staring at nothing through the slanting rain. Even so, we must go back, we must try, we must have faith. I am beginning to sound—and indeed to feel—like a Chekhov character; but then I seem to remember that Chekhov also loved picking mushrooms.

Long and Broad Novels

A SHARP DISTINCTION should be made between 'long novels' that simply go on and on, perhaps giving us the history of a family through several generations, and 'long novels' that are really 'broad novels', perhaps covering quite a short time but advancing, so to speak, on a wide front. Anybody who can write a novel at all ought to be able to do one of these lengthy family chronicles, which require simply persistence and patience. But the 'broad novel', which demands a great variety of scenes and backgrounds and a host of entertaining minor characters, is a very different matter: invention and vitality are essential to it. They may be only four or five times the length of an ordinary novel, but even when they are going well they are extremely taxing and exhausting. No wonder Dickens never lived to see sixty. Tolstoy did, of course, but then he was an unusually powerful man. (Turgenev was almost a giant but lacked, I think, the fiery energy a huge novel demands.) Aldous Huxley, in one of his letters, said that he himself had the wrong physique for a truly creative novelist, whom he saw as a stocky, barrel-chested type. Am I thinking of myself when I mention this? Certainly.

Colds in the Head

I HAVE A cold in the head: my nose runs, my eyes stream, and though I don't feel ill, I do feel miserable and rather angry. To my certain knowledge I have been suffering from colds in the head, at fairly regular intervals, during the whole of this century. I don't need an icy winter; I have

had them during our hottest summers. I have had them
on mountains and in deserts, sailing in luxury liners and
standing in the trenches. My father had these colds, so do
one or two of my children and grandchildren: they are the
Curse of the House of Priestley. Nothing on earth seems
to prevent them or cure them. And so far, landing on the
moon hasn't been any help.

Interviewing

A YOUNG MAN, interviewing me a few months ago, sent
me a copy of his piece, and it began: 'Mr J. B. Priestley
is a worried man.' No doubt he felt that this started him
off with a bang, but in fact it completely ruined his piece.
Nothing I said to him suggested that I was a worried man.
There could hardly be a worse description of me, unless he
began by saying that I was a tall, slender and remarkably
handsome man. Even though I deplore—and frequently denounce—what is happening in the world now, I am anything but a worrier. I neither look nor act worried, and as
people go nowadays I am an unusually relaxed character.
But then interviewing is now very badly done, far worse
than it used to be before the Second War. There are two
reasons for this: many interviewers have no shorthand and
have to depend, often disastrously, on their memory; the
more highly-paid 'depth' experts on the Sundays are thinking about themselves and not about you. Out of the hun-

dreds of interviewers I must have encountered, the best was George Bishop, who did theatrical notes at one time, I think, for the *Observer* and then later for the *Daily Telegraph*. George asked you sensible questions and then set down exactly your replies. If there is anybody in his class these days, I have not had the luck to meet him. The worst interviewers I have known have been in Australia, Canada and the US. In America I have had so-called interviews that were wild inventions from beginning to end, and in which I was apparently insulting everybody. They did me much harm, and there was no redress. Nor can I see that I was anywhere at fault, though I admit I have never been clever at handling the press.

The Very Old on TV

THE PEOPLE WHO have given me most pleasure, when interviewed on TV, have all been very old, like Gordon Craig or Casals. The reason is that being very old they don't give a damn; they are themselves, like it or lump it; they don't worry a moment about their public image or what the critics will say or what the programme planners will do about them. Most people who are not very old are obviously too anxious to please when they appear on TV. They offer us too many smiles and charming little tricks, are too intent on buttering us up, and are clearly not their ordinary selves but are giving a performance. As soon as they have an audience of millions, most politicians look and sound like motorcar salesmen.

Fans?

WHENEVER I AM moving around among people I constantly hear this kind of thing: 'My brother's a great fan of yours'; 'My wife's read every word you've written'; 'They're both tremendous admirers of your work'; and so on and so forth. All these fans, readers-of-every-word, tremendous admirers, I am sure, are exceptionally nice people. But unfortunately they all seem to be shy and quiet people. I never catch them bursting into print or grabbing a microphone to tell the world how enthusiastic they are.

Dreadful Thought

ENCOUNTERING, ON NO. 3 platform of Leamington Spa station, two Shakespearean actors I knew, they told me they were filming *A Midsummer Night's Dream*—*The Dream*, they always call it. Bully Bottom having been mentioned, I said, 'I played that part at school.' Then a dreadful thought came like a thunderclap. 'And perhaps I've been playing it ever since.'

Inner Places

IF I WERE asked to give a young man or woman a bit of advice taking only a minute or two, it would run as follows: Try to regard your states of mind as visits to places. Now I am in the angry place or the melancholy place or the misunderstood-by-everybody place. The point is, if you do this you don't identify yourself with these states of mind: they are not *you*. And it really works. I can't claim any credit for this psychological device, because I found it in *Living Time* by Maurice Nicoll, who in turn got it from Gurdjieff, frequently referred to as a black magician or a charlatan by people who know nothing about him.

Which Jack

IN MY MIDDLE teens my father and I didn't always agree, and more than once he told me that if I wasn't careful I would end up 'just a Jack-of-all-trades.' Later, long after his death, I thought how wrong he'd been. But now, when I am much older than he was when he died, I am not so sure. Though I am still inclined to remove that 'just'.

Avant Garde

THOUGH I HAVE risked experiments—rather more than I am generally credited with—both in plays and books, and I am not rigidly conservative in my tastes, I have always disliked the avant garde. (But what is the difference between a great artist doing something new and the avant garde? Well, to give quickly one example—I would say that the Cubists were avant garde and that Cézanne was not. I might add that to my mind Henry Moore is not—and never was—avant garde.) What is it then I dislike about the avant garde? To begin with, I feel it is always too much aware of its audience—'Now we're going to give you people a shock!' It asks for—just because it needs—wide disapproval. It largely exists in a café-manifesto atmosphere. When its patrons finally arrive, almost always they are rich and fashionable, determined to be on the cultural bandwagon. The great innovators in all the arts are too *serious* to join the avant garde. They are far too deeply concerned with their work to bother about striking attitudes in public places. Whereas, I suspect, only half the energy of the avant garde goes into its work. The other half goes into publicity and bull-baiting the public.

Individualism

MORE THAN ONCE I have been accused of inconsistency
(though I have never pretended to complete consistency)
because while I was prepared to favour some form of socialism, I was at the same time strongly individualistic. But
these do not cancel out: it seems to me that one demands
the other. In the economic area of life, in which we are
necessarily involved with other people, what used to be
called 'rugged individualism' is wrong, and always suggests
to me unscrupulous and ruthless tactics, brigandage,
piracy. And it is these men who so often denounce and try
to suppress individualism in the social and cultural areas
where it should flourish. We on our side, who know we
must give away some of our economic freedom, should be
all the more concerned to preserve and even increase our
non-economic freedom as individuals, determined to pro-
tect our civil liberties, and keeping a particularly sharp eye
on attempts to bully us by officials who wish to compel us
to do this, that and the other, merely for their own con-
venience.

Security

IF I HAD insisted—over fifty years ago—upon having the
security that everybody seems to want now, I would never

have become a professional writer at all. I turned down several safe academic jobs to become a freelance in London, and I had a wife, a child on its way, just fifty pounds and no expectations whatever. This was nothing of a challenge compared with what happened not long afterwards, when I had to work double shifts to pay for the tragedy that was closing in on me, but here I will merely record that nobody left me any money, I never borrowed any, never asked for any kind of grant, fellowship, bursary, professional or private charity, and that the only *security* I had came from working like hell. Which indeed was where I was living at the time.

Doubt about Modesty

ALMOST ALL THE best men I have known, generous-minded and life-enhancing types, may have had a great deal of inner humility but they have never tried to appear very modest in their ordinary talk, have never been afraid of blowing their own trumpet. On the other hand, a lot of men who have accepted—or had imposed upon them in boyhood—the old English public school style of careful modesty in speech, with much understatement, have behind their masks an appalling and impregnable conceit of themselves. If they do not blow their own trumpets it is because they feel you are not fit to listen to the performance.

Noble Idealists

JUNG WROTE: 'PEOPLE who have an exaggerated ethical ideal, who always think, feel, and act altruistically and idealistically, avenge themselves for their intolerable ideals by subtly planning maliciousness, which of course does not become conscious as such, but which leads to misunderstandings and unhappy situations.' I defy anybody who has spent time in progressive, reforming, protesting groups, to deny the truth of Jung's observation. In nearly all such groups there is at least one person, inspiring and leading them, whose tender conscience and enthusiastic devotion to good causes make us feel temporarily ashamed of our own large areas of indifference, laziness, love of pleasure. Yet in these same circles those 'misunderstandings and unhappy situations' do seem almost inevitably after a time to emerge, making us feel suspicious of our friends and dissatisfied with ourselves, as we meet the reproachful look of the noble self-sacrificing idealist.

Lost Summer for Writers

WHEN I REMEMBER my life as a writer in the 1920s and 1930s I begin to feel almost desolate now. True, I am getting on and have probably been around too long. Yet when I talk to younger writers, what they tell me proves that I am not simply being bamboozled by my age. They can hardly believe me when I explain how much more personal, how much warmer and cosier, a writer's life was in the twenties and thirties. When you had published a book or had a play running, letters arrived by the score, some of them coming from fellow writers, often your very distinguished elders. Your publishers were not merely running a business but were your friends, delighted to tell you how your book was selling, to ask you how your next book was coming along. The whole relationship was much closer. Your agents were not simply looking for large advances, they were *looking after you*. And you seemed far nearer then to your readers or playgoers. You lived in a smaller but far friendlier world, into which big business had not yet found its way. It is the difference between the handsome and convenient 'pocket books', which publishers cared about, and the paperbacks of today, so many 'titles' put through a computer.

Little Dons

LIKE MANY ANOTHER writer I have suffered at times from the elaborate condescension, the arrogance and intolerance, of dons. They will review a book by a writer much older than themselves as if it were an over-ambitious essay by a second-year student. They look down on us from invisible and, indeed, imaginary heights of achievement.

Being a fairly popular figure both here and abroad, I am probably fair game; but now and again they even give my wife, a sensitive writer who is also a scholar, the same treatment. It never seems to occur to them that we could have been dons too, that if we do not teach in universities, if we have no professorships or readerships, it is because we decided years ago in favour of another style of life. If in secret they dislike being dons and envy our freedom—and this is what their behaviour suggests—this is not our fault. We cannot help it if they preferred security to risk and adventure. And let me add that the great dons, now vanishing from the scene, do not behave in this fashion. It is the little dons I complain about, like so many corgis trotting up, hoping to nip your ankles.

English Hotel Food

I HAVE BEEN reading yet another complaint about the wretched, tasteless (but expensive) food served in so many English hotels. The trouble here is that there are too many dining rooms and too few chefs. Once again, sheer numbers are destroying quality in living. If an hotel has no chef in the kitchen it should abandon any attempt at 'cuisine' and dinners of four or five courses, all of them ill-conceived, undernourished and unsatisfying. When in my youth I walked the Yorkshire Dales and scrambled up and down the Lake District, four nights out of five my dinner consisted primarily of a huge dish of ham and eggs—and I asked for nothing better. Would I have swapped them for a dab of floury soup, a mysterious but equally floury fish, two slices of lamb as thin as a postcard and apologies for vegetables, drowned sponge cake and artificial cream served in some sort of wine glass, cheese as shiny and hard as a stage prop? Never, never! If an hotel can find a real chef and provide him with genuine materials—well and good! But if it can't, then it should drop all this dreary nonsense, and settle for one thumpingly good old-fashioned course. Back to ham and eggs. Or bribe some old woman to dish up a real steak-and-kidney pud. Or order some more butter and bake some big potatoes. Or if none of that is possible and the local shop is any good, send out for some fish and chips. At least one dam' good helping of something edible and nourishing. But not that soup, that fish, that attenuated entrée, that nonsense of a dessert, that wildly impudent bill for so much flour and water!

Nineteenth Century Best

SOMETIMES MY MIND wanders down the centuries, and I begin to compare them, asking myself which I would choose to live in, being allowed only one of them. Well, I was born in the nineteenth, though as late as 1894, so there may be some prejudice here. (By the way, I have noticed that many people discover a peculiar glamour in the decade of their birth. So my daughters who were born in the 1920s seem to be fascinated by that decade, one that leaves me almost stone cold.) Bias or no bias, my choice has been fixed for some time now on the nineteenth century. I know all about its miseries—the spread of industry at its worst, the dark streets crammed with over-worked and underfed proletarians, the cholera-ridden towns, its extremes of wealth and privilege and of helpless suffering— but it is still the century of my choice, and the one I would choose to live in, given a comfortable income and a robust constitution. A man with these advantages and safeguards —born, let us say, in 1820 and dying in 1895—would to my mind have had as good a life as Western Europe could have offered him at any period. If he had had a sound taste in literature, music, painting, what a wealth of wonderful new work he could have enjoyed! What a wealth too of great seminal new ideas! (This century has merely acted out, usually in the worst possible fashion, ideas it inherited from the nineteenth.) Remember too the extraordinary energy and self-confidence of our great-grandfathers. The rats were not yet gnawing at the roots of Western Man. Again, while industry and ugliness were spreading rapidly, the greater part of the countryside, both here and on the Continent, was still unspoilt. Foreign travel might be slower and more inconvenient than it is now, but it was infinitely more worth while, delighting the traveller instead of boring the tourist. Food and drink were still comparatively pure and wholesome, were not yet tasteless chemical concoctions. The twentieth century has been exciting in the wrong way, creating more and more confusion and noise, and increasingly fretting the nerves with hints of disaster and, more recently, doomsday. And the nineteenth century was a great time—probably the greatest ever—for writers. Just before Dickens set sail for the second time to lecture in America, he was given a vast public banquet. No living writer would be honoured in such a magnificent style. Indeed, I doubt if we are capable of organizing such a banquet. (I have attended several 'banquets' recently, and the food and wine were much worse than I have at home.) No, reader, *you* can travel at supersonic speeds, creep into buildings a mile high, take a trip to the moon; but if I can have that comfortable income and robust constitution, I would rather slip away, back into that tremendous, zestful, wonderfully creative nineteenth century.

True Strange Story

I MAKE NO claim to psychic power or anything of that kind. Yet the following story is true in every detail. A few years after the Second War I was staying with an old friend in New York. He was officially connected with the American Poetry Society and as he had to attend its annual prize-giving banquet, he took me along with him. He had to sit at a high top table with other officials of the Society and the poets who were to receive its awards. I was at one of the round tables below, sitting next to a pretty woman-friend of his. After half an hour or so, I said to her—and this was not a familiar ploy and I do not know why it came into my mind—'I propose to make one of those poets wink at me, and I'll try the fifth one from the left, that dark, heavy-set, sombre woman, obviously no winker.' After concentrating on her for a minute or two, it seemed to me that she winked at me, and I cried triumphantly, 'She did it. I'm sure she did.' But my neighbour did not believe me and I really was not sure myself, the top table being twenty or thirty feet away and the light not too good. However, after the speeches and awards had been made and we broke away from our tables, the dark, sombre woman poet, who had been one of the prize-winners, came up to me. 'You're Mr Priestley, aren't you? Well, I must apologize for winking at you. I've never done such a thing before and I can't imagine what made me do it then. Just a sudden silly impulse, I guess!' I told her quite truthfully that she had made me very proud and happy, and then somebody else claimed her. I have forgotten her name but I do remember that my New York friend told me, two or three years later, that she had just died, though only, I think in her early forties. I have never tried the experiment since, preferring to rest on this one triumph. Perhaps I ought to add here that I did not wink at her, just commanded her to wink at me. Also, I suspect that halfway through a boring public dinner, when everybody's mind is emptying, is probably the best time to attempt this feat.

After-Dinner Speeches

IN MY TIME I have had to make a great many after-dinner speeches, and as I have acquired a certain facility in this small and dubious art I am offering a little advice to any-body who has been asked to make an after-dinner speech. If you have a really bad voice, hard to hear even with a microphone, refuse the request. It is not your job. Then, unless you are a managing-director who has to include a lot of figures in his speech, do not write it out and then read it. The audience feels it is not being given your full attention, and soon becomes restive. Some speakers write out their speeches and then learn them by heart. This is certainly better than reading them, but it is rarely very successful. There is usually something wrong with the intonation and timing of the speech. Moreover, a speech carefully prepared in advance may be dead against the mood of the audience. I remember once being a guest-speaker at the annual banquet of a famous arts club. One of my fellow guests was that admirable dramatic critic, James Agate, who had conscientiously prepared a solemn talk about aesthetics. But an audience of painters and sculptors, many of them not quite sober, was in no mood to listen to a talk on aesthetics, so poor Agate's speech was a disaster. This is perhaps an extreme case, but I think any speaker is foolish if he does not make some allowance for the character and prevailing mood of his audience. He can do this of course if he merely uses notes. Experienced speakers, such as senior politicians, can often use notes very cleverly, but this requires practice. A speaker unused to notes is apt to lose the attention of the audience while he is fumbling the bits of paper in front of him. What then is left? Sheer improvisation? This takes some doing, though I must admit there have been many occasions when I have left everything to chance. If you are not entirely incapable of improvising anything, then I suggest you do what I generally do—that is, to have suitable odds and ends in your head, ready to be used if necessary, but then depend largely upon establishing a quick relationship with the audience, having guessed its mood. Be too short rather than too long. Nearly everybody goes on too long—'A last thought' and so forth. Again, if you don't tell funny stories to your friends, then don't attempt any in an after-dinner speech. No humour is better than failed humour. Finally, assume—as I always do—that after dinner most people want to chat with their neighbours at the table and don't really like listening to speeches. You are a nuisance, not a treat. Having told yourself that—get up and show them they're wrong. If the very notion of doing something of that sort makes you tremble days before the event, send a telegram to the Chairman saying you have gone down with flu.

Cold Conceit

I DON'T OBJECT to a kind of warm vanity in a man. Generally there is behind it a genuine humility. He shows off to prove his company is worth having: he is really trying to be hopeful about himself. But there is a certain sort of cold conceit, often found among some scientists and dons, legal men and senior civil servants, that has always been to me a complete barrier to any further acquaintance, let alone friendship. I cannot remember ever penetrating this cold conceit to discover the real man behind it. I may add that if

I instantly dislike such men, they too make it immediately clear they will never like me—and indeed have often made up their minds before ever being in the same room with me. Under the one roof, I play dog to their cat. Come to think of it, there is a good deal of warm vanity in most dogs. They too show off hoping to justify our acceptance of their company.

Fate of the Myths

NOW WE LIVE among the scummy wrecks of those great myths that for so long took possession of man's mind and soul. The Earthly Paradise is to be found on the beaches of the Bahamas and Jamaica. The technologists who write fatuous books about the year 2000 have plucked the Golden Age out of the past to set it in the near future. Avalon, where curiously beautiful maidens walk beneath unfading apple blossom, will soon turn up in southern California, a Disney enterprise. The shining heroes are divided between the City and Sports pages. The Silver-Shadow Rolls is almost a divine chariot. Magic potions may be obtained from the shop down the road, though some are on prescription. As for the Great Time of primitive men, beyond our little time of change and sorrow and death, we catch glimpses of it in TV advertisements with all their happy faces, their enchanted breakfast foods and soft drinks, the similing sorceries of their detergents washing whiter and whiter. . . .

No Good Shot Look

MY FRIEND Rupert Hart-Davis was chairman of some function at which I was guest of honour. 'Jack,' he said as we prepared to sit down together, 'why do you always look so miserable when you're about to be praised?' If there had been time for a proper reply, I might have mentioned—if I had thought of it—Phyllis Satterthwaite. The time was in the early 1930s when I played a lot of tennis (badly) and was a member of Queen's Club. I was playing a set of mixed doubles and my partner was Phyllis Satterthwaite, one of those country-house-and-Riviera perpetual tennis-and-bridge players, but a friendly soul. I had just done something rather good at the net, where I was always at my best, making the game ours. As I joined her at the baseline, she said quite pleasantly, entirely without malice, 'When you've played a good shot, don't *look as if you've played a good shot.*' And there, Mr Chairman, Sir Rupert, is your answer.

Britain's Contribution

WHEN WE BRITISH feel we are being grimly realistic about our economy and our place among the nations, we like to remind one another that 'The world doesn't owe Britain a living.' But in my opinion—though I don't say we should bank on it—the world *does* owe Britain a living. If the world were truly grateful and generous it would settle a handsome pension on us for the next half-century. Our contributions to world civilization should be suitably rewarded. I am not thinking now about our inventions and discoveries, though a formidable list of these would be easy to produce. What I have in mind now are all those Britons of the educated classes who lived on private incomes and had no desire to be manufacturers and salesmen, boosting the export trade. They went riding everywhere, often through the strangest places, mounted on their hobby-horses. It is they who told the world about its birds, its flowers, its gardens, its stones, its jungles, its more fantastic animals and fishes. Often they risked their lives, their fortunes and their domestic happiness, so that the world should know more about itself. Today, in one continent after another, innumerable universities, learned societies, schools, are deep in debt to us. So I declare once more —the world *does* owe Britain a living.

The Root is Fear

WE ARE ALWAYS reading and hearing that it is men's innate aggression that is responsible for the world of today. This is nonsense, and dangerous nonsense because it prevents our getting down to the root of the trouble. This is fear, and so far as modern man is aggressive it is because he is fearful. Almost all propaganda is designed to create fear. Heads of governments and their officials know that a frightened people is easier to govern, will forfeit rights it would otherwise defend, is less likely to demand a better life, and will agree to millions and millions being spent on 'Defence'. (The use of this term suggests it is fear not aggression that lies at the root.) Jung noted all this, years ago, and wrote:

> 'All one's neighbours are ruled by an uncontrolled and uncontrollable fear just like oneself. In lunatic asylums it is a well-known fact that patients are far more dangerous when suffering from fear than when moved by wrath or hatred.'

Even if he were not bedevilled by propaganda, modern man would still be fearful. There is so little that seems to be under his own control. He is at the mercy, he feels, of mysterious monsters.

Dish-into-Person

THE YOUNG WOMEN who read and note all that advice—and there seems to be more and more of it every year—about eye shadow and foundation cream and hair styles and fashion and diet and exercise must sometimes feel they are walking into a trap. If they are fairly normal, enterprising young women, they want to be regarded as 'a dish'. But a dish, first tempting and then, we hope, satisfying the appetite, is not a person. And most young women, including many professional super-dishes, have a passionate desire to be regarded and accepted by at least one suitable male as a person, highly individual and rather special. But dish-into-person and then at times person-back-into-dish—all this must be very tricky, confirming my opinion that it is much harder to be a woman than to be a man.

Science and the Future

HERE IS Peter Medawar declaring that 'The greatest liberation of thought achieved by the scientific revolution was to have given human beings a sense of a future in this world.' He goes on: 'The idea that the world has a virtually indeterminate future is a comparatively new one. Much of the philosophical speculation of three hundred years ago was clouded over by the thought that the world had run its course and was coming shortly to an end.' Quite so; but what about our own time here and now? It seems to me there are now far more people (including many of the young) whose minds are darkened by thoughts of doomsday than there ever were at any other time. And now it is not God who will destroy the world, it is ourselves. We can do it, seemingly, by nuclear war, by global pollution, an improvident use of our resources, the population explosion. Moreover, in all of this, science and technology have played a leading part. I am not denouncing science and technology, but I cannot help feeling that this is hardly the best time to boast about 'the liberation of thought achieved by the scientific revolution.' As for that 'sense of a future in this world', I would say that most intelligent men and women, not naturally pessimistic, are beginning to regard that future with horror. No doubt all is not lost, but science and technology will have to work hard and fast to start clearing up the mess they have made. And 'outer space', which Medawar sees in terms of 'a tremendous endeavour only just beginning', will not offer us much help. It is the state of this world and of our own 'inner space' that demand our attention—and, I add with respect, that of brilliant contemporaries like Sir Peter Medawar.

Mean about Paper

THE PIECE OF paper on which I am typing this note is a small end bit that I carefully cut off a sheet that had not been fully used. I did this because I am—and always have been—miserly about paper. (All except toilet paper: I am lavish in the loo.) There is no sense in this fear of wasting paper. I can't afford a yacht but I could easily afford a stationery cupboard crammed to its ceiling with typing paper of the best quality. As it is, I hate to see an unused half-sheet. Once, many years ago, I shared a London flat with a friend, really a poet, who had undertaken to write leading articles for a weekly. He would type an opening sentence or two, tear the sheets out of the machine until his room began to look as if it had known a snowfall, and I had to tell him he was driving me out of my mind.

All Too Happy

EVERY MONTH WE receive, without asking for it, a copy of a Soviet propaganda 'colour mag' called *Culture and Life*. It is filled with smiling faces. Everything is wonderful. Not a hint of a snag anywhere. And how stupid this is! Why not a few scowling or drooping faces? Why not include some grumbles from Siberia or somewhere? Why not a letter or two from our old acquaintances *Indignant* and *Disgusted*. It would be much better as propaganda, and I would begin to read the thing again.

Said Before?

IT IS POSSIBLE that something like this may be found somewhere among the Moral Maxims of Rochefoucauld,

but though I have them somewhere I am too lazy to look
them up—so here goes: We are never so attractive nor so
repulsive as we often imagine ourselves to be. What we
ignore is the idea that we may be just rather dull.

Positivist Vanity

I HAVE THOUGHT for a long time that all extreme posi-
tivists and rationalists are both inspired and fortified by an
unusual amount of intellectual vanity. This is some sort of
compensation for the rather arid and narrow universe they
have created for themselves. The rest of us—the 'woolly-
minded' to which I belong—are free of this vanity because
we feel there is so much that we don't know. We live in a
mysterious universe, indeed in a mysterious world, and
can only fumble towards an explanation of so much that
happens all round us. Of course we are sometimes taken in
and must then meet the gleam in the eye, the condescend-
ing smile, of those who knew all along it was nonsense.
But even so, in our humility we have more fun, live in an
infinitely richer universe, and are a few steps nearer wisdom. Moreover, those who have severely rationalized
their consciousness, ignoring all hints and warnings from
their unconscious, tend to behave, especially at times of
crisis, with the wildest irrationality. I could name well-
known names, but prefer to withhold exact evidence and to
remain vague, in my woolly-minded fashion.

Connolly Reversed

THANKS TO Cyril Connolly we all know about that thin
man who is screaming to be let out of a fat man. But what
if there are thin men haunted by the outline of a fat man,
with an impressive presence, an easy digestion, and plenty
of friends?

Victorian Glimpse

A GLIMPSE OF the last century. I am sitting on my grandfather's knee and we are in a horse bus. It is a cold winter's
night. I am fascinated by the thick straw on the floor, which
was there to keep people's feet warm. I remember nothing
about the other passengers, but then I was very young indeed, and I know very well that this must have been some
time in the 1890s. But I can still see that straw on the floor.

Disembodied Existence?

IN A REVIEW of a book by Professor H. H. Price, I read
that it is difficult to imagine 'a continued disembodied

existence.' (The subject under discussion is survival after death.) Now while I neither look nor sound like an essentially spiritual type, I can well imagine a continued disembodied existence, and indeed that is the life I lead when I am using my imagination. What I feel would seem horrible and terrible, a long nightmare, would be to leave such an existence to be 'embodied' again, to find oneself landed with a heavy carcase together with innumerable limitations, irritations, ailments, tied at last, as Yeats said, 'to a dying animal.' What a prospect!

Patience Please

IF I WERE allowed another life and also granted a virtue largely missing from my present existence, I would without any hesitation ask for patience. Except for the last few years—and I am not very sure about them—I have always been wildly impatient. I may have looked fairly stolid but inside, at work or away from it, I have always raged and blazed with impatience. It has been my curse both as a man and as a writer. I have lived at the opposite extreme from those meticulous colleagues, making full use of their gift of patience, who are ready to write something four or five times over again. All too often I have been only two-thirds of the way through when I have longed with passion to finish the job and get on with something else. As in work, so in life, when lack of patience has diminished my pleasure and made me seem carping and arrogant to other people. Now and again, in these last years, I have caught a glimpse of the sunlit garden where the patient take their ease. But only a glimpse—so it is still *Why doesn't this idiot ring me up?* and *Where the hell is that letter they promised me?* I tell you, if I am given another turn, God grant me patience!

Riposte At Last

IN THE EARLY 1950s I figured in a divorce case, though I was not called upon to give evidence and was not represented in court. This did not prevent the judge, notorious in legal circles for his love of publicity, from telling the world my conduct had been 'mean and contemptible', a conclusion based on slender evidence that he did not even understand. A large section of the English Press, almost gleefully, splashed this 'mean and contemptible' across its pages, doing the dirty on me in millions of homes. Now, looking back on my life, I realize that on innumerable occasions I must have behaved badly—being inconsiderate, bumptious, over-bearing, stupidly insensitive, as if determined to remain an adolescent lout. I plead guilty to a score of faults. Even so, after searching hard, I cannot recall an occasion when my conduct was mean and contemptible, nor do I remember anybody ever charging me with such conduct— until of course this judge had to speak his piece and fifty editors rushed his slander into print. And equally of course

I had to grin and bear it, having no means of redress. Now and again I still hear or read one of those after-dinner speeches telling us once more that our Law and our Press are close to perfection and the envy of all other nations, and I can't help wondering if we aren't being rather too complacent, too smug, too anxious to deceive ourselves. Or are such doubts characteristically mean and contemptible?

In Death Row

WE COMPLAIN ABOUT our behaviour in this world. But if, as so many people seem to believe, we are all living in Death Row, waiting for the morning of the execution, we don't do too badly.

A Braggy?

BELIEVE IT OR not—but in half a century of professional authorship I have never spent ten minutes planning a literary career or even wondering about one. I cannot prove this but at least I can add that since the end of the Second War I have refused a knighthood, a life-peerage, a C.H. Here I must stop because in another moment this entry will turn into what my children used to call 'the braggies'—to my shame.

Status Symbols?

ONE OF OUR close friends—and we are very fond of her—is always talking about 'status symbols', which she sees everywhere. Dealing only with them as clues, she is a kind of social detective, the triumphant sleuth in dining and drawing rooms. Yet when I look round this study, which is a fairly large room and anything but bare, being cluttered with all manner of things, I fail to see a single object that could be dismissed as a status symbol. I don't believe there is one here. But if I told our friend this, she might retort that a boast about the absence of status symbols is itself a status symbol. Madness lies this way. But then that may soon be regarded as a status symbol. Help, help!

Sound Men

I READ THAT a man recently appointed to an important post has figured for some years in a list of 'thoroughly sound men.' This does not surprise me. Our thoroughly sound men like to fill important posts with other thoroughly sound men. This guarantees that nothing bold and original, imaginative and life-enhancing will happen, that a hesitant timid muddling and shuffling will continue as before. It is only in wartime—and even then only when the country has been in danger for a year or so—that unsound men, odd cranky fellows, are given a chance. As soon as the war is over, the thoroughly sound men are again in command—if it can be called command. What is overlooked here is the fact that this country is always in danger, and that thoroughly sound attitudes and tactics can bring us closer and closer to ruin. For my part I would welcome, if only as a change, the arrival at 11 Downing Street, as Chancellor of the Exchequer, of some quite notorious crackpot.

What Do We Know?

THE WEAKNESS AND hollowness of a time when science is dominant can be easily understood. At such a time we think we know everything when in fact we know nothing. I refer here of course to questions of real importance. Who are we? What are we doing here? What will happen to us? What is *really* happening to us here and now? It is true that men in previous ages had no short and clear answers to such questions, but at least they did not pretend they knew everything but felt they were living in a mystery. True, the very idea of a mystery is a challenge to the scientist, and this is as it should be: we must not blame him. On the other hand, he must not behave as if he were a high priest of some dogmatic and bigoted new religion. He must not lose his temper, his manners, his sense of proportion, if some of us, making no great claim for ourselves, feel that now and again the veils of Time and Space have been briefly lifted. Sometimes he might tell himself, if only late at night, after a long day, that really we know nothing.

Writers as Company

APPEALS TO SET up hostels for visiting writers—or for places where English writers can meet—arrive here to find no warmth and the stoniest ground. After much experience both at home and abroad, I decided long ago that writers, taken as a group, are very poor company. They are in the word business and so don't want to waste too many. They are also extremely suspicious of one another and so inevitably tend to be cagey. Smith is determined not to let himself go when he notices that Brown, Jones and Robinson are present. In a small and fairly intimate group, there have been brilliant exceptions: Wells, suppressing nothing, could be very lively indeed; de la Mare was an enchanting companion; Hugh Walpole, in his more malicious and not wildly enthusiastic moods, could be very good value indeed; and Monty Mackenzie was a superb and tireless raconteur. But I would always rather take a chance with any collection of painters and musicians. And I ought to have put musicians first, if only because no matter how distinguished and hard-pressed they may be, they are almost always ready to make music. I think the best evenings I remember, at Cambridge, in London between the wars, in the Isle of Wight, where we had a fairly spacious hall that was all wood and wonderful for sound, were impromptu musical evenings when notable performers, relaxed after wine or whisky, played for the fun and private glory of it. And like most painters, the musicians could talk freely and amusingly. Moreover, while musicians and painters might be acquainted with jealousy, envy and malice, it seems to me that collectively they still have a warm regard for the dignity, honour and fellowship of their professions. All this appears to have vanished among British writers, who are now, so to speak, 'atomized'. It is as if most of them now felt defeated, and kept to themselves, nursing their wounds. And this has happened, I feel, only during the last twenty-five years or so.

National Health

WHEN OUR National Health Service was planned, it was naturally assumed that our people would be healthier than they used to be. National Health would therefore make fewer and fewer demands. But now we are told that we urgently need more and more hospitals, more and more doctors, more and more money to maintain the Service. From this we can draw two conclusions, different but equally disturbing. First, we have a society responsible for more and more illnesses, largely psychosomatic. Secondly, that our medical services are basically faulty, probably ignoring the root causes of illness because they are so busy with its symptoms, often hard at work preventing the body curing itself. (In some cases—and this happened to me a few years ago—murdering benevolent bacteria with an over-zealous and indeed ruthless use of antibiotics.) I may add that I think both conclusions are right, and that because I accept them it does not mean that I am an enemy of the National Health Service.

An Intuitive

STRICTLY SPEAKING, I don't think, and I don't believe I ever have done. I am capable of reflection and a certain amount of meditation, but the logical process of ratiocination has been denied me. Scores and scores of times I have gone for a solitary walk, intending to think hard about a novel or a play before settling down to work on it, and nothing worth remembering has happened. My mind has refused to stay with the subject. But then later, perhaps getting out of the bath, there has come a flash of intuition, giving me what I wanted. Even my opinions—and I am full of them—arrive intuitively, never after any hard careful thinking. Now more than fifty years ago, during my graduate year in Cambridge, when I had no more exams to bother about, I became fascinated by metaphysics, borrowing all manner of philosophers from the University Library —bless its generous heart! But I could never have been a serious student of philosophy: I lack the necessary equipment. And there is something else, to which I will return below. The reason I am considering these matters is that this afternoon, rummaging at the back of a bookshelf, I came across something I had not set eyes on for years and years: *Syllabus of a Course of Lectures delivered at Trinity College in Cambridge by J. Ellis McTaggart.* He was a gigantic character, and whatever my limitations in other directions I could enjoy such a character. As I re-read this *Syllabus* I was trapped all over again by McTaggart's argument, which I found it impossible to refute, as helpless now as I had been over fifty years ago. But now, just as then, I couldn't *believe* it. Thought might be trapped but intuition was still free. And that is as it always has been. Not at all an epicene type, nevertheless there seems to be a feminine creature bossing my mind, always telling me to stop trying to think because she will supply all necessary answers and conclusions.

Revolt

IF SOCIAL AND cultural revolt, as I have just read, 'is the form of our age', then fairly soon, though I may not live to see it, there will be nothing to revolt from except revolt.

By this time, everything that bored intelligent people in their youth will be back in fashion.

Difficult Question

CALL THIS A note on ageing. The man I have to live with—J.B. we will say—is rather wiser and more responsible than the J.B. of years ago. Naturally he no longer has the same creative energy and zest. But there is something else, I regret to add. Though I do my best to check this, I find him colder and meaner than he used to be, obviously running out of empathy. But who is this 'I' responsible for the unfavourable report? God—I hope—knows!

Western Answer

WHAT HAPPENS WHEN we are writing at our best, swiftly and surely, apparently without effort? (And in my experience, doing it without the help of a single drink.) Does somebody or something take us over, as I was once inclined to believe? Or is it that in sheer creativity we escape from the prison of the ego? Certainly at such times we forget ourselves completely, never for example giving a thought to critics and readers or audiences, being entirely free from egoism. And if this is so, then in our own way, through selfless imagination, we must be almost coming within sight of the goal promised by the gurus, teaching their disciples how to meditate. Perhaps this might be our Western answer to the Eastern mystics, our enlarging of consciousness in a cold climate.

Hard on Friendship

WHEN PEOPLE LIVE in small well-knit communities, I imagine that friends as they get older see more and more of one another. This is impossible with us and our friends. It is not that friendship itself decays. We are, I think, as eager to see one another as ever we were. But most of us are very busy people who have to do a good deal of travelling, so six months can slip away without a single evening being spent together. There is something very melancholy about this, especially as not one of us is young and healthy and anything might happen without our knowing about it. And indeed, I am writing this because a long-distance call has just told me that a man I have known fairly intimately for fifty years, a man I used to see every few days when we were much younger, is dying. There is something sadly wrong here. It is as if the conditions and demands of our society have taken a heart-warming circle of friendship and blown it to smithereens. Most of the persons I have in mind here are—and have been for some time—what is generally called 'successful'. But we have not been very successful in our friendships.

Anti-Ghoul

IN OUR INNER worlds are mountains, deserts, jungles, ruined cities, fallen temples, regions as barren as the moon, and sunlit blossoming valleys that we catch a glimpse of in our happier dreams. In these worlds live all kinds of creatures that we never feel we have created ourselves. But if we feed them they grow bigger and stronger, perhaps so powerful that they try to take us over. If we refuse them nourishment, then although they may never vanish they begin to droop and wither and power ebbs out of them. Among these creatures of the interior is Ghoul, for whom we are now providing a heyday. It is Ghoul who delights in blood streaming down, shinbones and heads being cracked, eyes being gouged out. And there are now some West End cinemas that are laying on lunch, tea, dinner and supper for Ghoul. In short, they are in the violence racket. Against any protest, they tell us their aim is catharsis. They rub our noses in the results of violence to discourage and not feed the Ghoul in us. But all the facts are against this argument. We have now had more than twenty years of increasingly brutal violence described or shown in cheap fiction, drama, TV programmes and films. If catharsis worked, then there ought to have been less and less violence in real life, whereas there has been more and more. I suggest that those of us who believe in civilization should make sure we don't help to feed Ghoul. Instead of saying, as so many people do, 'Well, I suppose I ought to see how far this film goes,' we should stay away until something less barbaric is announced. *Don't give the Ghoul-feeders, the violence caterers, any of your money*, because that, for all their talk of catharsis, is what they want.

The Complicators

AFTER LONG AND bitter experience I now find it easier to spot—and thus try to avoid—a *complicator*. This is a person who has an unconscious drive towards making all arrangements difficult. If you present a first-class complicator with a simple, sensible, practical plan, he will never accept it but will immediately introduce variations that can turn it into a nightmare. Suppose, for example, you have been foolish enough to promise to meet him at a London terminal, he will ring you up on a bad line from Devon to announce that he is not sure if the train he will take will arrive at Paddington or Waterloo. 'Better try Paddington first, I think,' he tells you, 'but of course it's just possible it may be Waterloo. Now listen—' And off he goes into a maze of daft arrangements. If he and his wife are coming by car to stay with you in the country, then the complicator is in his element. No time of arrival can be suggested: he has to pick up his wife at her sister's in Bucks; they have to call for a clock they bought somewhere near Banbury; and there is the problem of the clutch pedal that has been giving them trouble for weeks; so that you feel you are playing host in a novel by Kafka. Please notice I have assumed that the complicator is a male. About twenty-nine times out of thirty, I would guess, this is true. Women can be forgetful, hazy about time, given to sudden changes of mind, but in my experience they are rarely downright complicators. They may be whimsical, sometimes to test your devotion, but they are rarely at the mercy of their unconscious drives, as a certain kind of man is. I think he insists upon complication because any simple straightforward arrangement bores him. He wants life to be difficult. He enjoys moving stealthily along the edge of nightmare. And I have realized for years now that he is a pest.

A Book to Bring Back

THERE ARE SOME books it is dangerous for me to open, simply because I go on reading them, though I have read them before, when I ought to be doing something else. This has just happened to me with A. G. MacDonell's *Napoleon and his Marshals*. I cannot understand the fate of this extraordinarily fascinating book. A few years ago, staying with an American friend at Martha's Vineyard, I described it to him and said I would send him a copy when I returned to England. But then I was told that the book had been long out of print. (It was published in 1934.) I have just looked up MacDonell in the *Everyman Dictionary of Literary Biography*, and found to my astonishment that while half-a-dozen of his books are mentioned, *Napoleon and his Marshals*, far better than anything else he ever did, has been left out. I knew and liked Archie MacDonell but thought his *England, their England* and other satirical novels fairly lightweight stuff. He was a high-coloured, hot-tempered Highlander, and I well remember telling him in 1940 that the BBC would welcome him back, though afraid of his hair-trigger temper. 'Me? Bad-tempered?' he shouted, purple in the face, 'What the devil are they talking about?' (He died in 1941.) What he did in *Napoleon and his Marshals* was to take the solemnity, pomp and military pedantry out of the Napoleonic Wars and put in their place a novelist's sense of character (the Marshals themselves were an odd collection), drama and humour and humanity. It is easier to understand and enjoy the whole crazy epic of those years here in this book than in any other I know. We have often been told that good books eventually find their way to most of the readers who would appreciate them, and while this is comforting I am afraid it is simply not true. What about *Napoleon and his Marshals*?

Not a Brass Farthing

JUST OCCASIONALLY, WHEN I had nothing better to think about, I used to wonder whether, as a writer, I was over-rated or under-rated. Now, during the last two minutes, I realize that I no longer give this question a thought, not caring a damn either way.

Importance of the Maigrets

I HAVE AN idea that Simenon, whose work I have enjoyed for many years, prefers the novels or tales he writes without the help of Maigret. And if so, then in my opinion he is wrong. Without Maigret—and indeed Madame Maigret too—he would have never reached his tremendous international reputation. I am not thinking now about detection, for after all the detecting and the puzzle element in Simenon are hardly fascinating. What we enjoy are his odds and ends of people, his creation of atmosphere, his ability to convey—under all weathers from sleet to burning afternoons—a sense of deepening uneasiness, of despair and corruption, of ruined innocence and crawling evil. But if the Maigrets are absent, it is a picture without highlights. They are essential to the scene. They represent what almost all the other people have lost, namely a steady triumphant goodness. If we had a Maigret who took bribes from his wealthier suspects, a Madame Maigret who was having an affair with a handsome young man during the Inspector's absences, the tales would soon be intolerable. Moreover, being a fundamentally good human being, Maigret takes understanding and compassion into a world, the dark under-

side of Paris, in which understanding and compassion seem
to have been lost along the way. Without the Maigrets,
Simenon would be just another clever pessimistic contemporary novelist. It is their underlying simplicity—we might
add their *innocence*—that completes and heightens the
scene.

Empathy and Comic Characters

THIS NOTE—AFTER observing a distinguished critic making heavy weather out of the difference between the comic
characters of Shakespeare and those of Ben Jonson. We
might say—cutting it short—that Shakespeare *likes* his
comic characters and Jonson obviously doesn't. But we
need not be quite so peremptory. We can try to enlarge the
comparison, perhaps picking up a few little windfalls along
the way. Clearly Shakespeare has empathy to spare and
Jonson hasn't. Jonson is ready to stand his chief comic
characters round after round of verbal magnificence, that is,
before he has done with them and they find themselves
dumb in his dry harsh world. When he is ready to create a
few comic characters—with Falstaff their inspiring leader,
the Falstaff whose brutal dismissal is Jonsonian not Shakespearean—Shakespeare has in mind a world very different
from Jonson's, a world that is expansive, without rigid
boundaries and narrow conclusions, where even a fool or a
self-important dolt may flourish in his own fashion, where

[51]

the sun can shine for all. It is impossible, I imagine, for an arrogant scholarly man, embittered by frustrated ambition, to create such an easy tolerant world or to enjoy its more absurd creatures. These demand not only creative energy but also a certain fundamental humility. It seems to me that this kind of world and the wide-ranging empathy needed to people it are very hard to find in contemporary fiction. Alienation, loss of identity, self-pity, contempt for everybody not of one's own sort, a feeling that your very readers are not to be trusted, a feeling that never troubled the great primary writers—some or all of these factors have conspired to rob today's novels of the very qualities, both empathic and mythopoeic, that would satisfy so many readers. This explains the undeserved success of those 'big' machine-made and synthetic novels, and the decay of fiction among an intelligent and imaginative readership.

Writing Plays

WRITERS NEW TO the Theatre should be warned that when their plays are produced they stand naked in the marketplace as they never do with any other form of authorship. Moreover, if the play is a 'flop'—and all dramatists have had their 'flops'—then the author, facing all the people who have worked so hard for him, cannot help feeling responsible and ashamed, however brave a face he may put on it. Not long ago, an experienced, successful, very clever novelist, wanting to write plays and not getting them right, asked my advice. I began by pointing out that the drama is comparatively a coarse medium, if only because it demands that every night you interest and move several hundred people of all sorts. And as soon as you choose this medium, you must armour and toughen yourself. Nobody brought more sensitivity to the Theatre than Chekhov, but even so he understood all this very well.

Poverty No Joke

BEFORE THE FIRST War many youngish serious writers believed it was their duty to stay poor, content to count pennies and exist in extreme frugality. But conditions favoured this plan then. In my later teens I would gladly have left my wool office, to live in a cottage (rent 9d) and write, if I could have counted upon a pound a week. From about 1920 until the present and monstrously overpriced day, poverty in England has been no joke. It is in fact a bad country to be poor in. To begin with, it is too cold and wet, robbed of the sunshine and warmth that are the friends of the poor. Fuel and stout clothing have to be bought. Again, cheap food in England is nearly always wretched stuff. (In America, when I knew it best, cheap food—Navy Bean Soup at the drugstore, and the like—was excellent: it was the expensive food that was a fraud.) And tradition of decent and even honourable poverty had vanished. A frugal cleanliness was on its way out. No doubt there are English 'drop-outs' who have returned some way towards the idea of deliberate poverty that influenced serious young writers sixty years ago. But unlike those writers—or painters or musicians—the new poor do not seem to be doing much with their leisure and liberty. They may be 'doing their own thing' except that all too often their own thing seems to be more or less the group thing. In short, they quit the herd only to join another once.

All the Goings-on

DOWN HERE IN Alveston, what rescues me from the depression—almost descending into a Samuel-Beckett-ish fashionable despair—that I feel in London is the weekly arrival of the *Stratford-upon-Avon Herald*. Mind you, this is no escapist sheet. It copes with reality—as for example *Estranged Husband Smashes Front Door Glass With Spade*; or, turning from private to public life, *Three Years and Still Waiting for Playfield*. Even so it might be reporting another country in another age. For instance, in the reading matter arriving in or from London, marriage seems to be on the way out, and there are gloomy pieces asking us to abandon the idea of family life. But any week you have only to look at photographs (not bad) in our *Herald* to see smiling brides and grooms—mark this—all manner of parents and children illustrating the continuity, the affectionate pride, of family life. Marriage and family on the way out—Are you kidding? Then almost every week I am astounded by reports of what is happening all round me. Dismiss the idea of people sitting at home, listless or goggle-eyed in front of TV. Why, with all our goings-on, there can hardly be anybody under seventy-five sitting at home. Merely to look at the photographs and glance down the reports makes me feel dizzy. Coffee Mornings (whatever they are), public luncheons, afternoon meetings, cocktail or cheese-and-wine parties, official dinners, presentations of prizes (for anything, everything), staff parties, lectures, concerts and amateur theatricals, and dances—*some in fancy dress*, so you would think Charles II, Louis XV and the Prince Regent were still busy anywhere between Snitterfield and Shipston. The Women's Institutes alone—and there seem to be scores of them—are listening to talks about everything from Abstinence to Zen, or competing like mad with cakes, pies and flower arrangements. Then again, people turn up from the ends of the earth because they once lived in Stratford, and are photographed, stiffish perhaps but smiling, shaking hands with the Mayor. And I may add that most of these meetings and parties and prize-givings seem to cut right across class divisions, just as this lively, communal life, with its enthusiasm and zest, banishes the idea of the contemporary English as a lot of lazy, sullen, bloody-minded TV-trapped idiots. (Not long ago, round here in a week we raised several thousand pounds to buy a local schoolgirl the kidney machine that saved her life.) Sometimes I think the politicians and their commentators blame us for their own lack of imagination and empathy.

The Dummies

I WAS SOMEWHERE in my middle teens and I was walking along Lumb Lane, Manningham, Bradford, and for the first time ever I came to a halt outside the secondhand furniture shop there. Not only did I stop but I stared in amazement. In place of the usual Victorian junk, its window was filled with ventriloquists' dummies, all staring back at me. I bought one of the cheapest of them, with no body, just a head with its various strings. After several futile attempts to bring that dummy to life, I believe I swopped it for a one-string fiddle—in fashion then among us chumps—that I found easier to master than ventriloquism. But this meant that ventriloquial acts continued to fascinate me, as they do to this day. It is not the jokes I care about, for they are not often very good jokes; it is the dummies. The truth is, after the first minute or two I no longer regard them as puppets manipulated by the ventriloquist. They seem to me to have a life of their own. It is a life different from ours, for I feel they belong to some gnomish race, in touch with us only intermittently, and always exasperated and indignant at our lack of understanding, their bold and roving eyes appearing to glitter with fury, their strange voices rising in protest or deepening into despair. An invitation to sing, which is something they usually do very badly, placates them only for a very brief period, and then they remember how frustrated they feel. This is not entirely our fault; their gnomish society seems to have no comfortable middle class; it is divided between upper class swells who wear monocles through which they ogle lasciviously any girls in the audience, and, at the opposite extreme, members of an irreverent and pugnacious lower class, hoarsely deriding any attempt by the ventriloquist to suggest better manners. But of course it is just possible that there does exist, in their gnome society, a sensible middle class that stays below somewhere, always refusing to exhibit its members in any place of entertainment, disdaining all those hearty and often *risqué* jokes and not even being tempted by invitations to contribute a song.

Medical Puritans

THE TYPICAL PURITAN hates pleasure and would put a stop to it if he could. But anything to do with business and making money has his respect, perhaps even his affection. And now that we are always having medical opinion quoted at us, it is time we noticed that a great many doctors—and especially those who like to see themselves in print—have a strong puritanical bias. It is our pleasure they denounce. Their ideal is a very rich man who has never smoked, has never drunk anything but distilled water and fruit juices, lives on salads without any dressing, and by spending half the day and part of the night at the telephone gets richer and richer. This used to be true only in America but now we have medical men who take the same miserable line. I remember, a few years ago, there was published a report by a group of doctors on a hundred important New York executives. The doctors found that they smoked too much, drank too much, ate too much rich food, and stayed up too late. It was their pleasures that were threatening their lives. But nothing was said about their commuting, perhaps twenty miles in, then another twenty back again, or about the five telephones on their desks, or about those terrible deadlines with the Board and the ruthless competitiveness and the dread of the future—No, sir, that's just the way business is. It's also just the way puritanism is.

Authors and Others

READING A PUBLISHER'S memoirs I find myself being told once again that authors are very peculiar people. Having read or heard this too many times, I must do a worm-turn and declare that it is nonsense. Of course there are some odd fish among authors, but so there are among members of other professions. Indeed, my experience suggests that architects, musicians, lawyers, doctors, military men, parsons, editors and publishers have a larger share of eccentrics, crackpots, chuckleheads, loobies and drivellers than authors have. And there is a good reason why this should be so. Authors are primarily interested in conduct and motives. They are better acquainted with their own minds than most men are. They are less inclined to give way to self-deception. They keep an eye, so to speak, on their unconscious. If they appear to be very peculiar, I would say that nine times out of ten they are putting it on for effect, no doubt feeling it is expected of them. Now dining out has frequently taken me into the company of the 'hard-headed', the industrialists, the business men, the entrepreneurs, and once the wine has gone round and round then out come the neuroses, the aberrations, the daft eccentricities, the startling crackpottery. After all, a man must be half-dotty to call himself 'hard-headed'. We authors have no pretensions in the carapace-head department, but I will let slip a professional secret: we are inclined to be *hard-hearted*. Somewhere beyond the glow of compassion and the coloured mists of fine writing there is all too often a thick hard frost.

Russian Visitor

FROM CHEKHOV'S NOTEBOOKS: 'Everything which the old cannot enjoy is forbidden or is considered wrong.' In its own time, this was an acute observation. But now we would have to reverse it, declaring that Everything that the young cannot fully enjoy is no longer worth bothering about, is finished—*out*. I took the Chekhov quotation from a translation made by S. S. Koteliansky and Leonard Woolf for the Hogarth Press. I knew them both but cannot remember ever seeing them together. They must have made a rum pair of collaborators. Leonard Woolf was one of the *steadiest* and most sensible men I have known, designed by Jehovah to be Virginia's husband and a director of the *New*

Statesman when Kingsley Martin was its editor. (I was a fellow director so had a continuing taste of his quality.) Koteliansky might have wandered out of a play by Chekhov. He arrived on a student's visit to England before the First War, then stayed here the rest of his life, existing very frugally but cheerfully on odd bits of translation and reading for publishers. His English was fluent but delivered with a thick Russian accent. He detested writers who were affected and insincere, denouncing them for what he called *Showin' Goff*. As he seemed to enjoy my company, he must have thought me free from *Showin' Goff*. I liked him enormously, but I lost touch with him during his later, and I am afraid, much lonelier years. This was entirely my fault—I was just being too dam' busy—and now for a long time I have been sorry, ashamed of myself and all this blasted unrewarding busyness. But perhaps among the dead who are dead to us but not to themselves, he may be keeping a sardonic eye and ear on the *Showin' Goffers*.

An Old Bad Policy

CHANCELLORS OF THE Exchequer might try bearing in mind one reason why we British dislike our governments. No matter what party may be in power, the very things that encourage sociability and easy optimistic talk are taxed with the utmost ferocity. I refer of course to drink and tobacco, which together help to break down our reserve with one another, bring out the gregarious strain in us, promote hospitality, and set the late evenings glowing. My parents—and I am going back sixty years now—had many friends who were always popping in, and this was no severe strain on their budget when tobacco was fivepence an ounce, threepenny and fourpenny cigars not to be despised, and whisky three-and-six a bottle. But one greedy foolish government after another piled duty on duty until we arrived at a time, also suffering from the communal cancer of inflation, when only the rich and the improvident feel at ease entertaining their friends and fellow-sufferers. And men not at ease enjoy cursing the government.

Better Outside

THERE WAS FOG about, and through the window the day looked cold without being crisp, rather like a dish rag left out all night. However, there were letters to be posted, so off I went. And for the ten-thousandth time, once I was out of the house I found the day much better than I thought it would be. This is a tribute to the English climate. In so many places, from Bangkok to Oslo, or Lima (Peru) to Winnipeg, it is even worse outside than you thought it would be. Only in England—and specially in Alveston, Warwickshire can you cheer yourself up by exchanging slippers for walking shoes and then closing the front door behind you.

Not a Good Combination

IN CEYLON, ON the road between Kandy and Matale, we saw an elephant and a lorry trying to cope with a very thick and heavy log. What happened in the end, I don't know, but while we looked on no progress was being made. It might have been sensible to try either two elephants or two lorries. And there was something about this odd wayside scene that suggested the melancholy bewilderment of Asia and Africa, continually adding lorry to elephant but not getting anywhere in particular.

Size of the Universe

BETTER MEN HAVE been appalled by the thought of the immensities of space, the unimaginable size of the universe. But let every man speak for himself. Whenever I read or hear about the millions and millions of stars in our galaxy, and the millions of other galaxies, my heart leaps up at once: I am filled with joy. Nothing cheap and mean about *our* universe! No threat of satiety here. And though our earth may be only a speck in it—and I myself only a speck on a speck—there is something in me that longs to cry aloud its wonder, gratitude, and sudden happiness. So don't be afraid, Gentlemen of the Telescope—do me a favour! Make it billions and billions of stars in our galaxy and a billion other galaxies.

Seasons

I CANNOT UNDERSTAND all those people who save up—
or swindle the shareholders—to spend their remaining
years in places that have no seasons. There they are—saying Goodbye for Ever to Spring, Summer, Autumn, Winter,
with all their variety, their conjuring to please the eye, their
delicious season of fruits and vegetables. What is the use
of having asparagus in December and strawberries in
February if all flavour has vanished? Who in his senses—
sun or no sun—wants every month to seem like every
other month, days you can neither look forward to nor
regret, a life that cannot escape from looking like a coloured
advertisement? They couldn't pay me to lead such an existence, altogether without seasoning.

Things

AMONG THE IMBECILITIES of our society is its attitude
towards things. Never in the history of our species have
more things been produced. Almost everything from the
planet's future to a decent peace of mind is being sacrificed
to more and more and more things things things. It is as
if we were turning ourselves into a bigger sort of insect
fixed into an idiot pattern of manufacture and distribution.
Yet at the same time we care less about things themselves

than our grandfathers or our forefathers did. Few of us really try to understand things, to take proper care of them, to cherish and love them. Once past childhood, which at least appreciates some things, increasingly we pay things less and less real attention, seeing them as so much disposable stuff. If we are up-to-the-minute types, then we are already planning to rid ourselves of the boring wretched things we possess in order to welcome into the house whole vanloads of new bright things things things.

My Two Heroes

A NOTE ON my long comic novel, *The Image Men*. Now clearly it represents an attempt to bring into contemporary writing the old leisurely *picaresque* tale that has always fascinated me. This does not mean that it is out of date. In fact it was—and still is, as I write this—very much up to date, if only because it satirizes so much that belongs to our age—notably academic life and especially its social sciences, the mass media, big business and our present style of politics. So much will be obvious to any intelligent reader. But something else I attempted seems to have been missed. My two central characters, Saltana and Tuby, are introduced as if they were failed academics turning themselves into cynical con men. But they develop into what I shall call true heroes, able to swing the narrative over from the fashionable negative into the positive, in which a fair measure of faith, hope and charity triumphs over despair, nihilism and utter pessimism. Saltana and Tuby may be regarded to some extent as comic characters; but they are heroes, not anti-heroes. And the positive values and qualities they come to embody, before we have done with them, are not brought in to please the idle-minded reader: they are the values and qualities I cling to in my own life. The absence of trendy darkness and despair does not mean that I know less about living, in all its aspects, than these younger writers do. There are fairly long odds on my knowing a great deal more, my experience having been longer, wider and thicker. Parts of it have demanded faith and hope and a certain amount of courage, including the courage to be a literary man who has never tried to cater to fashionable literary opinion. If this leaves me outside somewhere, I can't grumble, if only because I have never liked the sight, sound and smell of so much that is inside, cherished by weekly reviewers, young lecturers in Eng. Lit., and the fancier publishers' cocktail parties, but rarely accepted, I have noticed, by master mariners, night nurses and other people who have seen and endured a lot of this life.

Not the State Please!

INCREASINGLY I MISTRUST and dislike large-scale capitalism and I am ready to welcome various forms of common ownership. But I don't want State Socialism. This is because I detest the State. It is a bully and a cheat. It compels or at least encourages its bureaucrats to behave badly. If I owe it money it insists upon my paying interest, but not a penny of interest comes my way if it owes me money. It is always mannerless and surly, and though I have paid it a fortune in taxes I never remember even seeing the ghost of a *Thank You*. On the other hand, it doesn't hesitate to send me letters dark with suspicion and snarling in tone. I am sure the men who sign these letters are courteous and pleasant in their private lives, but in office hours they are working for the Big Bully. Again, the State is such a vast and complicated organization that it cannot help being slow, cumbersome, wasteful. To hand almost everything over to this monster would be like trying to run a farm with dinosaurs. Socialism if necessary—Yes. But with the State taking it over—a thousand times *No*.

The Great Song

IN WRITING THIS I have in mind not professional musicians but ordinary members of the concert-going and record-playing public. And I wonder how many of them share a fancy of mine that has haunted me on and off for years. This is what happens. I am listening, let us say, to Verdi's *Falstaff*, and not, I must add, for the first time. But now I am suddenly bewitched by two themes that come flashing out of the score, lasting only a few moments. I have to track them down on a recording and then play them over and over again. And this has happened with other music, some of it on a higher level, some on a lower level, than *Falstaff*. Certain phrases not only delight my ear but seem to have a special meaning for me personally. It is as if there existed a *Great Song*, never to be fully revealed to me, only to be heard in varying snatches; and as soon as I hear one of these I am entranced. What the *Great Song* would do to me, I cannot imagine. Perhaps it would bring home to me all of my life worth recording. Perhaps as the world's noises leave my dying ears, the odd snatches and patches of the *Great Song* will come together and take their rightful places, and as all the lights fade until my eyes know only darkness, my ears, always better than my eyes, will be finally and magically ravished by that elusive *Great Song*. All just an odd fancy of course, but even so more nourishing, more rewarding, than what medical men, economists, politicians are reported to be saying.

A Teasing Riddle

LET US SAY I am lying on the big sofa in my study, reading something I find rather dull. My mind drifts away from the printed page and I am about to fall asleep. But what happens then is that a train of thought enters my mind. It does not bring with it a load of nonsensical stuff. What is being thought is apparently quite sensible. But it has nothing whatever to do with me. Nor is it the kind of thought I could associate with my wife or anybody else living in this house. It is just as if my mind, somewhere between waking and sleeping, has picked up, as a twiddled radio set might pick up a strange programme, what someone else, not known to me, is but thinking. When full consciousness is returning there is a moment when I remember what has been going through my head and tell myself that none of it has meant anything to me. Finally, there is no dream effect about these alien trains of thought, and they never suggest anything wild and silly. They are not unlike what one hears on a crossed telephone line. But they remain a teasing riddle.

The Division in Huxley

REVIEWERS OF Aldous Huxley's *Letters* have been telling us what a kind, gentle, sympathetic soul he was. My own acquaintance with him over the years was very slight, but I certainly agree with this account of him *as a man*. But out of his writing, especially his novels, a very different figure emerges. As a novelist I would say he was far from kind and gentle, often quite cruel, and generally unsympathetic to the characters he borrowed from real life, sometimes savagely caricaturing them. This division between the man and the writer is fairly common. A man will write constantly out of what seems the blackest despair, forcing his pessimism upon us, and yet his friends will tell us he is in fact wonderful company, delightful to be with, gay and affectionate among his intimates. For my part, I don't like this dichotomy, far commoner now than it was in earlier ages. I feel that earlier writers—especially the major writers—did not divide themselves in this fashion. They didn't keep one self for their work and another self for their friends. They were more or less all of a piece, going easily from life to literature, literature to life, so that in both you met the whole man. In Aldous Huxley's case, I would say that the personality encountered in his letters or in his company was close to his real self, and that as an intellectual novelist, aware of his reputation, he could not help following fashion—hence the savage caricatures, the occasional cruelty, the grotesque sexual incidents. He was all the more likely to do this because he was not naturally a novelist at all, and if he had been starting to write during the last twenty years I doubt if he would have produced a single novel.

Among Politicians

I NEVER FEEL at home in the company of professional politicians, not even when I have known them for many years. This is chiefly because on their two main levels we cannot meet at all. On the level of ideas, speculations, wandering thought, intuitive feeling about the world, their profession compels them to over-simplify everything, so that we might say they produce headlines and posters instead of drawings and paintings. This does not mean that they are really quite simple persons. On the level below, largely out of my sight because I do not see life in such terms, they seem to be deeply and often subtly engaged in a power chess-game, appallingly complicated because they are making moves not only against their opponents in other political parties but also continually against their own colleagues. So on one level they are too simple and on the other too deep and devious for me.

A Note on 'Q'

HAVING TO MOVE some books I came upon a neat set in blue binding: Dent's complete *Duchy Edition of the Tales and Romances of Sir Arthur Quiller-Couch—'Q'*. He had been my professor when I was up at Cambridge and we became fairly well acquainted, even though he cannot have enjoyed my ruthless parody of his lecturing style. However, towards the end of my last term, when I already had my degree and had done some coaching for my college, he asked me to stay on to lecture and so forth. I thanked him but said I had already refused several academic jobs, having decided to go to London and freelance there. He said that was exactly what he had done, leaving Oxford for Fleet Street or thereabouts. I never saw him again until the later 1930s, when I found myself sitting next to him—we were both down to speak—at a publisher's dinner, and then he made me laugh and I made him laugh—'no problem', as people like to say, because he had a tremendous sense of humour. And he needed it if and when he considered the final phase of his literary career. His lectures, artful performances playing to packed houses, were immediately successful when published as *The Art of Writing*, *The Art of Reading*, and so on; but he was not really a first-class critic, far inferior to his friend Walter Raleigh at Oxford. On the other hand, as a story-teller he was largely forgotten, and this complete edition of his fiction, arriving too late, was received in a fashion that must have greatly disappointed him. Yet the best of it, to readers who know how to ignore fashion, is far more rewarding than his criticism. And indeed his last novel, *Foe-Farrell*, first published in 1918 and deeply influenced by the War (though it is not a war novel), still deserves more attention than it has received so far. Somebody ought to discover it, perhaps for television, which needs a few discoveries.

Daughters

AFTER CHEKHOV, THAT wise man, had visited the Tolstoy family he cried in effect, 'Daughters are the thing!' It was

Tolstoy's daughters, loving but also sharply observant and realistic, who had given him the best account of the great man. And the most satisfying theatrical biographies of recent times that I know are both by daughters. They are *Gerald* by Daphne du Maurier, and *Freddy Lonsdale* by his daughter Mrs Frances Donaldson. Both men were rather difficult quirky characters, and not a single absurdity or piece of self-indulgence is missed by these sharp-eyed ladies, yet their unwearied affection and their pride in what these fathers accomplished shine through the text. Certainly, in these two biographies, daughters are the thing!

Nature

BECAUSE I AM no longer any use to her, Nature resents my existence, cluttering up her scene, and so keeps sharply punishing me—with cramps and aches and the rest. She will probably do me in fairly soon. Life at my age is like staying at a certain Scottish castle, with Lady Macbeth smiling her goodnight and adding sweetly she hopes I have everything I want. And I will admit that in order to keep going I demand help from that very science at which I have taken an occasional swipe; with the result that when I go to bed I have to go into such a routine of medicaments that I wake myself up, after yawning and nodding and napping through one TV programme after another. Even so, while acknowledging the scientists' magical pills and ointments, I am still on Nature's side, which I am sure represents the feminine half of the universe. And because she is Woman on a gigantic scale, we should be very very careful how we treat her. A pill or two here, an ointment there, she will pass, I feel, but there is a limit to her tolerance. As soon as she thinks she is being scorned, she will take her revenge. Just when we imagine we are cheating her, she will cheat the hell out of us. Try to force her and her creatures—so many unfortunate cousins of ours— into the food-factory business, and soon you will be eating the factory and missing the food.

Class

SOCIAL CRITICS FROM abroad who don't really understand England and the English nearly always make one assumption that is quite wrong. They assume that our class system is imposed from above. And it is not. It is imposed from within. Whatever they may say, however much they may protest, the English instinctively favour a class sytem. If they find themselves in a situation in which class is no longer at work, they will proceed to make it work, not feeling comfortable without it. I have noticed this over and over again. I don't say this will go on and on. Indeed, there are signs that it may now be weakening, chiefly because of recent changes in styles of life, dress, accents, among the young. Even so, the English class

system will outlast me, for one. It will be some years before
we feel more comfortable and at ease without it than with it.
And we still drag in *Class* where we would be much better
without it. A good example can be found in travel.

If it were left to me, I would abolish tomorrow the term
Class from any description of seats in planes and trains. On
any but the shortest journeys I insist upon travelling *First
Class*. My reason for doing this has nothing whatever to do
with social status. I am a wide man, plagued with gout and
attacks of cramp, and I need a wide seat. In any second-
class compartment that is full, or as the man in the middle
in those horrible tourist seats for three in planes, I suffer
and will probably make other people suffer. If I was asked
how I was travelling and could say 'Wide seat', everybody
would understand. But if I have to mutter 'First Class' I
feel embarrassed because the hearer might imagine I think
myself a cut above the company of ordinary sensible people,
whereas as a rule they provide better company.

The Gourmets

CERTAINLY MEN WHO neither know nor care what they
are eating or drinking easily forfeit our respect. But some
of us are beginning to pull well away, in our irritation,
from the people at the other extreme—the exquisite tasters,
the vintage snobs, the *three-star Michelin* gourmets. There
is, we feel, a decent area somewhere between boiled carrots

and Deluga caviaro, sour plonk and Château Lafite, where we can take care of our gullets and bellies without worshipping them.

Chez Whitaker

IT IS ALWAYS at this time of year that I remember I haven't yet taken even a peep into the new edition of *Whitaker's Almanack*. So now I have just finished dipping into its ocean of facts—1220 pages of close print, incidentally well worth the £2 that Whitaker, no profit-at-any-cost-of-decency man, charges for them. But even after saying this, I must add that once again, for the umpteenth time, I can't help noticing how little space in this vast compilation my friends and I occupy. Let's face it—we aren't Whitaker people. If we all dropped dead this year, I doubt if more than an inch of next year's edition would be devoted to the lot of us. We are just not *Almanack-In-people*.

But my reading isn't so much egoism. I like to learn something—not much, but something. For instance, a rather idle page-turning introduced me to the Republic of Rwanda, busy exporting hides, extract of quinine and pyrethrum flowers. It has been a member of the United Nations for the last ten years, and in its capital Kigali (4,273) no doubt there is some good talk about international relations and world affairs. It has a British Ambassador, though not in residence there. And after all that's *something*, isn't it?

Existential

A FILM NOTICE reads, 'In one basic sense, it is an existential film, dealing with man's inability to know others or be known by them as anything more than an object . . .' Would I have spotted this if I had been there? Do I know how an existential film differs from a non-existential film? In my youth I read, purely for pleasure, a great deal of philosophy, but that was before existentialism came out. Determined to catch up at last, I have just been poking around in a dictionary of philosophy, looking up the various existentialists. But I would still not risk using *existential* as a description of a novel, play or film. And I am so thick, so insensitive, that I never seem to have shared Heidegger's *angst* or Sartre's nausea, except when I have been suffering from food poisoning. And now I can't help feeling, in a fusty-musty way, that all too often *existential* is just slipped in to add a bit of tone, an extra flavour, another guinea's worth of communication in depth.

That's another thing I've been left out of—this new *angst* and nausea and desperation about *communicating*, out of which a few chaps seem to be doing very nicely. When I was learning how to write, I didn't even realize I was trying to get into the communicating business, and so I was spared much anxiety and grief. A few years ago, at a crowded party, I met for the first time one of our most energetic younger playwrights, who had told my wife he was a fan of mine. But after regarding me sombrely for a few moments, he said, 'I can't communicate with you.' Could this have been an existentialist moment?

Not for Me

THERE IS ONE matter in which I sharply differ from people who may be close friends of mine. They can spend night after night happily having their opinions confirmed—and indeed, often shouted at them—and feasting on their own propaganda. It is almost as if they were bringing their own bath water for another baptism. I find this hard to understand. If I have made up my mind about an important issue —for instance, nuclear weapons or the Vietnam War— and have given my opinions a wide public airing, I don't want to keep on attending plays and films about nuclear weapons or the Vietnam War. I might possibly try a play or a film that was in favour of these horrors, just to discover if it could produce anything that could shake my conviction. But to go for a night out to a theatre or a cinema, and then, so to speak, be only attending your own meetings all over again—this is not for me.

Scott's Journal

WHILE I WAS searching a high shelf for another book, my fine old Edinburgh edition of Walter Scott's *Journal* would not be denied, and I found myself at pasture in Vol. II. Scott is a queer case. (I may add here what I have often declared—that his fiction, especially his 18th-century tales,

is now sadly underrated.) His High Toryism, Scots snob-
bery, medieval nonsense, leave me cold. In almost all his
major decisions, he behaved foolishly: for example, to
keep his fiction anonymous, to create and maintain the
monstrous Abbotsford, to go into a huge publishing
gamble with Ballantyne. And he could deplore his taste for
'desultory reading', when in fact it was the making of him.
Scott all wrong, then? Yet I have only to begin going
through the *Journal* again to feel that this is the man for
me, with every page deepening my affection. He does not
lose me even when he complains, as well he might—what
with his lameness and rheumatic headaches, social duties
and terrifying author's commitments:

> January 13. 1829. The day of return to Edinburgh is
> come. I don't know why, but I am more happy at the
> change than usual. I am not working hard, and it is what
> I ought to do, and must do. Every hour of laziness cries
> fie upon me. But there is a perplexing sinking of the
> heart which one cannot always overcome. At such times
> I have wished myself a clerk, quill-driving for twopence
> per page. You have at least application, and that is all
> that is necessary, whereas unless your lively faculties are
> awake and propitious, your application will do you as
> little good as if you strained your sinews to lift Arthur's
> Seat . . .

The heart goes out to him. Some allowance must be made
for ill health, but even so I find it odd to realize that he was
only then fifty-eight whereas at this moment I can give him
over 20 years. But then, in his place, I would have dropped
out of the social round he inflicted upon himself. Incidentally, until I began re-reading the *Journal*, I had forgotten

that ho and his friends regularly smoked cigars, something
I think I missed in my Regency book.

Old Notebook

FOR THE FIRST time for many a month I have been dipping
into my old notebook. This is a smallish but fattish notebook, with a shiny black cover, that until lately was never
far away from me for over 40 years. If I had an idea that
seemed worth considering—usually, though not always,
for a play—the barest possible outline of it went into this
notebook. A few of these entries became plays, but, looking
through them again, I am surprised to find that most of my
best-known plays never made a first appearance among
these notes. (Probably because I tended to use this notebook for ideas that didn't demand my immediate attention
and were often soon forgotten. There was a strong element
of the fantastic in many of them.) All together there must
be well over fifty unused ideas still sheltering behind the
shiny black cover. As tasting samples I offer the very first
entry and then the very last:

*Boat Day—miscellaneous crowd including young man who
wishes to go, young man just arrived, woman looking for
husband etc. Two or three acts. Club in tropics.*

This was the first, and now here is the last:

*Mountain Hut on frontier—those trying to get into Utopia
—and those trying to get out.*

And now, not without a touch of melancholy, I close the notebook and put it away—into its retirement.

Think Tanks

WHEN I HAVE to listen to somebody from one of those American 'think tanks', I cannot help remembering that verdict of the *Tao Te Ching*: 'Extreme cleverness is as bad as stupidity.'

Those Figures

WHAT ABOUT THOSE figures that keep coming out of the dark into the lighted area of consciousness, threatening me if I refuse to welcome them or holding out round white arms? They may vanish into their native darkness, but soon, very soon, they will be back again, called out by a paragraph in a newspaper or a few remarks overheard at a party. And I know some of their names too well—for example, *Envy, Jealousy, Malice, Spite, Big Sneer, Slander Hard*, and *Cut Down for a Giggle*. . . .

Youth and the Arts

THERE ARE TIMES when the Arts pages of certain news-papers and periodicals irritate me. The exasperation I feel is not on my own behalf but on that of any colleagues of mine in the arts who happen to be over fifty. (If pressed I might even say 'over forty'.) For these Arts pages—and indeed various TV programmes—are so determinedly devoted to youth and its avant garde. A few grey hairs—and you are *out*. And it is at these times that I remember an ancient Hebrew proverb I once read. It runs: 'There are many old camels that are laden with the hides of young camels.' I suggest that editors and TV programme producers might occasionally give this proverb a thought.

The Happy Woman

WHEN THE TALK at the dinner party turned to happiness, I declared that it couldn't be sensibly pursued, that nobody should expect to be happy, that it was only when one looked back that a certain time could be seen glowing with happiness. Then the middle-aged American woman sitting on my right took me up very sharply. 'Why, that's all wrong,' she cried. '*I'm* happy. I've *always* been happy.' And so forth. Yet the face she showed me, though hand-some enough, contradicted every word she said. Its innumerable fine lines never arrived from years and years of happiness. What she seemed to show me was a battlefield on which happiness—or even an easy contentment—had fought and lost.

Darbies and Joans

HAVE YOU EVER observed that the most enduring and warmly satisfying sexual relationships are so often between men and women who seem to most of us completely unattractive? It is not the handsome man and the beautiful woman who turn into Darby and Joan. At least four times out of five, I would guess, Joan has always been noticeably plain and Darby downright ugly. And I don't believe that their deepening devotion is simply rooted in gratitude, though it may have been nourished originally by wonder.

Bombing

WE HUMANS DON'T bomb one another 'back into the Stone Age,' as a few be-medalled idiots like to boast. No, not at all. All the records, including now many different nations, seem to prove that we bomb one another into better behaviour. Monstrous as it may seem, the bombs bring with them a new feeling for the common good, a surprising cheerfulness (and I write as one of the bombed), a compassion largely missing when nights weren't black and dangerous, a helpful spirit that departs after the victory parades. I am not referring now of course to H-bombs, designed to turn whole countries into radio-active cemeteries, to sentence the living earth itself to death. No better behaviour can arrive with them; and sometimes I have thought, after shouting myself hoarse denouncing the evil things, that somewhere behind their manufacture and stockpiling there lurked a huge deathwish, a hatred of life and a desire to wipe it off this planet. But some occasional ordinary bombing would do the English some good—and might bring America out of its sad dream of itself.

Snowed In

AT TEATIME THIS afternoon, before we had drawn the curtains, I looked up from the *Times* crossword puzzle to see that while there was still a patch of pale cerulean high in the south-east corner of the window, everywhere else it was snowing. Instantly, just for a moment, I was restored to the magic world of childhood. Magic and childhood apart, I tend to associate snow with my youth, when I lived among the hills of the West Riding, and winter came much earlier—and much harder—than it does now, and three years out of four there would be heavy falls of snow around Christmas. (If we are all deceiving ourselves about this, then why is there so much snow on Christmas cards?) Even so, the only time I found myself completely snowed up was as late as February 1947. I was living in a fairly remote old house called Billingham Manor (said to be haunted) in the Isle of Wight. There was no nonsense about this snowed-upness. The one road to and from the house was blocked, utterly impassable; nothing could be delivered; the telephone lines were down; and for about a week we were cut off, sealed off, lost to the world. I passed the time writing a play over which I had been brooding for a month or two, and I had finished it when the road was clear again. It was called *The Linden Tree* and, with Sybil Thorndyke and Lewis Casson leading the cast at the Duchess Theatre, it was an immediate 'smash hit'. But some of the credit must go to that astonishing snow storm in February.

Retort

AN ACQUAINTANCE IN Stratford this afternoon said, 'How are you, Mr Priestley?' I replied as usual, 'Old and fat.' 'You said that the last time I asked you,' he declared. 'Well there you are,' I told him. 'Now I'm old, fat *and* repetitive.' But is that the way to win friends and influence people? Probably not.

Something Missed

TOWARDS THE END of a longish life I now realize that what I have wanted all along—or at least from early manhood—is something I shall never have. That is to be a member of a small intimate community of persons who, though individually they may have separate strong interests (they may be writers, painters, musicians, philosophers, doctors), happily share a great deal of common ground. These people are both neighbours and close friends. We entertain one another frequently and always without ceremony, often taking 'pot luck' and keeping well away from the conventional dinner party. We would be able to create an almost instantaneous audience for a new piece of music, a display of recent paintings, a reading of poems or an act of a play, a philosophical discussion. It is not that I have no good friends or don't know any such people. I have and I do. But there is no hope of their living just round the corner, turning into neighbours, creating this dream community. On the whole I have been a lucky fellow, having been given a large helping of what I wanted—but not this, never this, though it has been at the back of my mind for over half a century. The term *nostalgia* has been very loosely and all too often applied to me and my work. (So, for example, a novel like *Lost Empires*, very much a symbolic narrative, had *nostalgia* daubed all over it, when in fact it was not nostalgic at all.) I suspect that the *Heimwey* element in my work, so far as it exists at all, is born of a longing for this home I have never had—and now never will have. True, the home I did have during my boyhood, warmed by my parents' free-and-easy circle of friends, for ever popping in and out, contributed to this longing, even though the people concerned were very different from those in my imaginary little community. But there is something else, deepening the regret, and it is almost as if I had known this style of life in some existence, have been haunted by it and so waiting, decade after decade for it to return. And now I know it never will. . . .

Bad Traveller

IT IS A fact that I have done an enormous amount of travelling, and on a planetary scale too, round the world and all over it. But before you dismiss this as yet another helping of brag—please read on. It is also a fact that I am a very bad traveller, no more 'seasoned' than a leg of lamb straight from the butcher. To begin with, I am a time-table fusspot, with a horror of arriving at the plane, the train, the ship, with only a few minutes to spare. Travel with me and you spend hours waiting for your transport. I detest arriving at hotels, with the exception of a happy few that don't seem like hotels. While prepared to lay out preposterous sums on first-class fares between places five thousand miles apart, I am almost miserly when it comes to daily expenditure, and can darken an evening because the price of a glass of Scotch seems ruinous. (I can't be dragged into a night club *anywhere*.) There may be heredity here, for my father, who enjoyed frugality, would carry heavy bags along fifty streets, during an August heat wave, rather than waste money on a taxi. But what makes me irritable, often downright bad-tempered, is something my father never knew. This is the idiot palaver with passports, visas, health certificates and the rest, turning us travellers into the humiliated victims of bureaucracy. (And it is far worse in the East than in the West. We taught them this nonsense, and so, out of sheer malice, they overdo it.) Shuddering yet I can recall chasms of this imbecility, as when, for example, in order to leave Bangkok to spend half a day in Cambodia I filled in form after form, including one that demanded my mother's maiden name. Again, when our plane landed to re-fuel in one Eastern city we had been given a form bristling with useless questions, one of them being *Are you carrying a weapon?* This was too much for my wife, who, behind a gravely beautiful exterior, is capable of daft high spirits, and she wrote: *Yes. Atom Bomb.* (This was before hijacking.) But when not tormenting bureaucrats, she remains serene, always arriving and departing graciously—unlike her fussy, irritable, growling Jack, that unseasoned world traveller always making the worst of it.

Going—Then and Now

IN 1856 PEACOCK's old novel, *Melincourt*, was reprinted and he wrote a new preface for it. Observing the changes that had taken place, he wrote:

'Thirty-nine years ago, steamboats were just coming into action, and the railway locomotive was not even thought of. Now everybody goes everywhere: going for the sake of going, and rejoicing in the rapidity with which they accomplish nothing. . . . '

If he could spend just half a day in our age of the internal combustion engine, when millions and millions every week-end set out just because they own a car, not knowing or caring where they are going, Thomas Love Peacock would be out of his mind.

A Wrong View of Literature

W E S E E M T O have been told over and over again, during the last thirty years or so, that real literature—as distinct from mere entertainment—contains a large autobiographical element and is indeed more or less disguised autobiography. Taking literature as a whole, I believe this judgment to be quite wrong. It may be true for our age, haunted by psycho-analysis and admiring above all else a certain intensity. But this emphasis on autobiography in fiction and, to a lesser extent, drama seems to me a sign of decadence. Perhaps it explains the lack of great *primary* writers, the giant creators, a Rabelais, a Shakespeare, a Cervantes, or indeed a Tolstoy or a Dickens, who add worlds of their own to ours, all out of an immense store of creative energy and zest. (Proust, undoubtedly a great twentieth-century novelist, may appear to reinforce the autobiographical argument, but a closer examination reveals his power as an original creator, all his chief characters, from Charlus to Françoise, being masterly creations.) And something ought to be said here about this use of 'entertainment' in a pejorative sense. Though the great primary writers offer us much more than entertainment, it is also true that in fact they don't hesitate to entertain us, not seeing themselves as authors of 'set books' for Eng. Lit. courses, appealing to the world and not to examiners and students. The fiction and drama that last longest come to us out of larger-than-life and not out of neurotic odder-than-life. They are born of imaginative breadth and generosity and not of do-it-yourself psycho-therapy. They are created when the ego is forgotten and not when it dominates the scene, as it does in work based on autobiography. This fashionable view of literature, I repeat, is quite wrong, and I believe it to have done much harm.

Starved Imagination

THAT WISE IRISHMAN, 'A. E.', wrote this: 'The power of imagination in national life might be the subject of a great book. It is the despised faculty among the vast mass of people, who do not realize how much their whole life is ordered by imagination, a spell cast on them by some enchanter who raised up in their hearts the image of a nation, a civilization or social order.'

Now everything may be different here in England by the time these words arrive in print. But as we stand now, as I write this, we are a nation continually wounding itself, with one section snarling and tearing at any other section, because its imagination has been starved. Nothing lifts it above the dusty political arena. If the people have been squashed into seeing themselves as consumers, so many pay-packet spenders, it is because their political leaders do not appeal from imagination to imagination. Such leaders might be right to consult economists, but when they are addressing the people they should forget the economists and try to make use of such imaginative powers as they possess. If we had faced 1940 in our present state of mind, with the imagination turned off and greed and selfishness turned on, we would not only have accepted Hitler's peace offer but in our reply would have asked him at once for a loan, probably through a Swiss bank.

Tough Guy

MANY YEARS AGO, Percy Wyndham Lewis decided to produce a portfolio of drawings of well-known people. He invited me to sit for one of these drawings. A friend of mine, who knew Wyndham Lewis, gravely warned me that this was a very tough aggressive fellow. I said that I would bear that in mind, but that I was a fairly tough aggressive fellow myself. The result was that the drawing of me was described in the artist's notes as 'the pugnacious face of the best-seller'. (And *best-seller* be damned! Wyndham Lewis was also a writer and he ought to have done better than this booksellers' term.) What I did was to call his bluff. I am not—and never have been—a tough aggressive type, not even during my years in the army. And I am convinced that Wyndham Lewis himself was not—and never had been—a tough aggressive type. He was really a neurotic fellow putting on an act. Of course I was putting on an act too, but not because I was neurotic but simply because I was playing psychological poker. I think now that Wyndham Lewis, who was certainly gifted, was one of those men who easily run out of luck, partly because he gambled with his gifts instead of steadily making the most of them. Every few years, somebody re-discovers him as a great neglected writer, but the reading public takes little or no notice. Somehow it knows better. It might be said to be continually calling his bluff.

The Mixture

WHEN I SPENT a good deal of time in America, I always smoked *Hayward Mixture*, originally recommended to me by an old friend who lived in New York, even though this mixture came from the Middle West. It is not as good as the best of our English mixtures, but even so, when a friend occasionally lets me have a tin of it, I smoke it with a peculiar joy. This is because its particular taste and fragrance immediately return me to America in the years I knew it best. Once again I am walking briskly through the canyons of New York; I am in a compartment of some long-distance American train, wailing across so many dramatic changes of scenery; and, best of all, I am back again, writing, painting or just wandering about, in the glorious Arizona desert, for which I can occasionally feel homesick.

The Bird Trappers

SMALL ITEMS FROM the nineteenth century. Our house was quite a small one but the front of it was thickly covered with ivy and possibly (I don't know) various creepers. Two men arrived with what seemed to me then a gigantic net. I can remember thinking they were bossy men, not nice at all. They put their net up, covering the front of the house, and were just beginning to make a noise, to frighten the birds into the net, when my father, who had been out when they arrived, came striding back. Though both public-spirited and compassionate, my father was also (unlike me) hot-tempered and instantly combative. He had those men and their bird-trapping net out of there in about one minute flat. And I don't ever remember seeing them and their like again. Perhaps they vanished with the nineteenth century.

More Money Than Sense

WE ARE ALWAYS being told that the rich are getting richer.
I don't know if this is true or not. I am not a financial man
and anyhow I don't move among the rich. What I *do* know
to be true is that now there are more and more people who
—in the old North-country phrase—'have more money than
sense'. These people buy things just because they are expensive. The advertisers have such people in mind when they no
longer bother telling us that their goods are the best,
having various unique qualities. Oh—no, they simply announce that what they are trying to sell is the *most expensive*.
Just that! They know very well that they have now a fairly
large public of affluent imbeciles.

Old Age

IF THERE HAPPENED to be a *Senile Courier* (*Incorporating
The Geriatric Monitor*) the following notes might be contributed to it by one J.B.P.

Tendency to delay putting on trousers because one foot
is standing on braces. Odd recent behaviour of pipes
scattering sparks and hot ashes on carpets and lapels of
coats. Going upstairs for something and forgetting on the
way what on earth it was. Remembering in detail the face,
voice, name, habits, of a man met in 1909 but no clues to

the man who called last week and is coming again this afternoon. Inability to wade through important leading articles. Growing horror of stag parties, whether pompous or drunken, and sharp preference for feminine company, though not in large groups. Distinct signs of nausea produced by the sight and sound of shaggy young men playing electric guitars and belting out one idiotic phrase over and over again. A deepening conviction that all money not spent on wines and spirits, fine cigars and tobacco, is just money wasted. No temptation to linger over advertisements in colour mags showing stern young men wearing expensive new clothes—or indeed those girl models who look like boys who have just had an electric shock. No desire to be IN except, mostly, indoors. Blank attitude, either as viewer or potential performer, towards TV *chat* programmes. Dislike of composers who reject the symphony orchestra— one of our noblest achievements, in favour of some weird daft collection of instruments all their own. Refusal to take any more literature as bed reading, with increasing preference for old 1930s detective stories. Desire to avoid the company of other grumpy old men, with all their monstrous prejudices. Fondness for taking glimpses of my earlier selves and then wondering how I came to be tolerated at all—but then was I ? Heart-warming love, hardly known to my younger self, of sky scenery, sunsets, gathering storm clouds, those palest and clearest blues that belong to the kingdom of Heaven. Constant dialogues with Death, of whom I am not afraid, though I shrink with terror at the idea of those doctors who would want to keep me alive at the expense of all dignity and decency. Finally, something I never knew in earlier years, the blessed feeling, coming through occasionally like some snatch of a heavenly song, the blessed feeling of *conscious love*. What a prize for fumbling and bewildered old age!

The Protectors

I DISLIKE COMMUNISM, having seen it at work in many places that nobody was allowed to get out of, and I have often expressed this dislike. Even so, I find I always mistrust those public men who are for ever loud and busy protecting me from Communism, who see the Red peril everywhere, and rarely suggest any improvement in our own society. These are the very fellows who are almost always ready to bring into our society the methods and practices we detest in Communism. What they are really denouncing is any country in which it is impossible to cash American Express cheques.

The Ascetics

SOMETHING I HAVE noticed for more than half a lifetime. Well-known men who boast they never drink or smoke are almost always the victims of less genial vices, namely, a boundless vanity and a passion for publicity. (Consider Bernard Shaw.) What a superb cigar, tin of choice tobacco, a Mouton Rothschild, or a bottle of old malt whisky, is to us low fellows, a newsman's notebook or camera is to them. Our weaknesses preserve a certain humility in us while theirs increase arrogance and armour-plate their egos.

Strange Malignity

I AM THINKING about that 'motiveless malignity' which Coleridge attributed to Iago, and which some contemporary directors of *Othello*—stupidly, in my opinion—have diminished by providing it with motives. Over and over again in my own life I seem to have encountered that same motiveless malignity. First let me say that I have always been surprised—and secretly delighted—when people have appeared to take to me at once. But the reverse—with delight turning to pained bewilderment—has happened throughout my life, with people apparently hating me at sight, for no reason I could ever discover. It goes as far back as the Infants School I attended, where a woman teacher—and I can see her square face now—was for ever singling me out to humiliate me and make me cry, so that I dreaded entering her classroom. (And with small children, there seems no possible end to such torment.) And ever since then in other schools, in an office, in the army, in Fleet Street, in the world of books and the Theatre, there have been these people, of both sexes, who seemed to detest me at first sight and did everything they could to make me feel the sting and weight of their malice. In all these instances, I could never discover any particular reason for their instant but enduring detestation and enmity. Such examples must not be confused with relationships that suffered from cross-purposes or false reporting of what I had said or done. Explanation could put these relationships right. But for the other sort, with bitter dislike mysteriously deep-rooted from the first, I could never find any excuse or reason. It was as if one of us was a cat and the other a dog. We might have been deadly enemies in some previous existence. Or as if my aura at once clashed with their auras. I shall be told that probably my dislike of them showed itself at least as soon as their dislike of me. But searching my memory as sharply and honestly as one can, it does seem to me that these motiveless malignants began it first, that my dislike was always a reaction. Before I quit the scene, I would enjoy a frank talk with one of them —I think.

Condolence

UPON LEARNING OF the death of men I have known fairly well, I always write, as soon as possible, a warmly sympathetic letter to their widows. During the last ten years, I would say that I have received no reply to about half these letters. I cannot help feeling that these silent widows—together with those who ask publicly for 'No letters'—are making a mistake. It seems to me that reading letters of condolence and then replying to them give a woman something to do during a time of grief and bewilderment. The dreadful wound is not re-opened but, so to speak, bandaged. Moreover, such exchanges of letters help to preserve a sense of continuity in our lives. But then I happen to believe that in these lives we are not being carried, on the conveyor-belt of passing-time, towards final extinction. We are highly selfconscious men and women, not cattle in a Chicago meat-packing plant.

Not Naturalistic

NOT ONCE OR twice but several times I have been described —and then pooh-poohed or severely denounced—as a naturalistic dramatist, like another Galsworthy or Maugham. This is idiotic. It makes me feel that these people can have seen or read only half of my first acts, which certainly seem naturalistic enough. But in all my major plays—and indeed some of my minor ones too—after a dullish conventional opening then something strange begins to happen and naturalism starts to fade away. All these fairly ordinary characters find themselves trapped into fantastic situations, impossible to discover among genuinely naturalistic dramatists. Now I ask the reader to accept this point, otherwise I would have to describe all these plays and be off on a false trail. And what I want to do here is to face and answer this question—Why did I go to work in this fashion? Why this conventional realism, these solid sets, these fairly ordinary people, the dullish talk, the lack of any attempt at heightened language? Why not raise the curtain on a fantastic situation, beginning with a bang? I will ignore any artistic reasons—though they exist—and declare emphatically that I had to keep in mind the prejudices of the audiences in the 1930s and 1940s, especially those members of the audience who were paying most for their seats. I had to lure them into my experiments, making them feel quite cosy at first. 'What? You—calling yourself an artist —could think like that!' Yes, madam, I could and wisely did. Remember, when I was working in the Theatre, it received no public subsidies—and indeed its patrons had to pay Entertainment Tax on their seats. A dramatist has to have audiences (not readers) or he has worked in vain. Unlike novelists, lyric poets, essayists and critics, a dramatist—if he has any sense at all—has to keep an eye on what is practicable. And if he does this he will be following the example of his masters—let us say, Shakespeare, Molière or Ibsen and Chekhov—yes even Chekhov, whose life and letters I know very well. (Incidentally, I cannot think of any *major* dramatist who did not succeed and become popular during his own lifetime: there have been no van Goghs of the Theatre.) We must also remember that conditions governing theatrical production have greatly changed during the last twenty years or so. A young experimental dramatist can now submit his work to certain companies enjoying enormous public subsidies or, at the other extreme, to tiny enterprises, 'working on a shoe string', that will risk producing almost anything at almost any hour from lunchtime to midnight. But conditions were very different when I was writing plays. I had to begin them cunningly to make the best of my time and place. But only an idiot would consider me a naturalistic dramatist. I was a wild one only pretending to be a tame one. In some respects I still am.

Faint Carpet Figure

HAVE I FOUND for myself 'the figure in the carpet'? This is the situation. I have been reading, pleasurably and profitably, Gordon Rattray Taylor's new revised version of his *The Angel Makers*. A fine book indeed, like all his others, though I still wish he had been a Jungian instead of a Freudian. However, here is the passage that made me ask questions of myself:

> But while the Romantics were undoubtedly matrists, equally undoubtedly there were other factors at work in their personalities which are not present in matrism as we find it in other periods in history—for instance the tough, aggressive matrism of the early Celts. The most noticeable of these, perhaps, is the element of nostalgia and longing, the sense of something lost. Since what the matrist loves is the mother-figure, the clue to follow here seemed to be to ask whether, in some sense or other, the Romantics had lost their mother. . . .

Now Susan Cooper in her book about me, and various

critics in passing, have discovered in my work more than fleeting traces of that 'element of nostalgia and longing, the sense of something lost.' And they have suggested, influenced no doubt by my novel *Bright Day* and my autobiographical *Margin Released*, that it was the First War that was responsible. What had been lost and what was being longed for was the world or the England or the West Riding before that War. Against this I have never openly protested, though privately I had never thought it to be quite right. It never rang a bell in me. But it now seems to me that the real explanation is simpler while on a deeper level. In actuality I lost my mother, who must have died when I was a tiny infant, so that I have no memory of her at all. After some years I acquired a step-mother, who, defying all legends, was kind, gentle, loving; but the fact remains that during babyhood and the earliest years of childhood, I had no mother. Too much should not be made of this. After all—if I may put it in these terms—for every ounce of nostalgia and longing in my work there are several pounds of humorous realism; and I am a long way removed from any typical Romantic. But no doubt a certain faint *figure in the carpet* can now be detected and explained; and I have done it myself.

The Sauciest Dress

MANY PEOPLE WILL be surprised to learn that the most saucily provocative dress that girls have ever worn was the crinoline. The popular notion that it was the prudish choice of a prudish age is nonsense. It came from the Paris of the Second Empire, though the Empress made it fashionable in order to benefit the French textiles trade, the crinoline demanding huge lengths of material. No doubt also that solidly respectable ladies took care that their crinolines should behave properly. But saucy young women, who knew they had attractive legs, had other ideas. They had only to make a little swinging motion or allow a brisk wind to do its work, then the young men walking behind them were offered enchanting glimpses. This is feminine provocation at its peak. Compared with the crinoline, covering everything from one angle and revealing almost everything from another, demure at one moment and naughty at another, our mini skirts are only a frank stare when compared with a bright-eyed flashing glance. Even in my temporary role of a lewd old codger, I don't suggest the crinoline should be tried out again—it was wildly inconvenient in its own time and would be impossible now —but I do suggest that when we talk so much about being *sexy* and dismiss the 1860s as strait-laced and prudish, we might give a thought to the crinoline.

New Edwardian Toffs

POSSIBLY A FANCIFUL idea—but let us see. Certain sections of our working class are now fairly affluent. And so many workers and their families felt ready for a new style

of life but found it hard to create one of their own. Then
why not imitate one that their grandfathers and grand-
mothers had always envied? This would have to be the
Edwardian upper class; certainly not the middle class, with
its books and concerts and dreary debates. Now the
Edwardian upper class rode about in motorcars, when
hardly anybody else did. So our more affluent workers
insisted upon buying motorcars, even when they had very
little use for them. The Edwardian toffs went abroad for
their holidays, so Dad and Mum, Bert and Glad, must go
abroad too. That lot went to casinos to play roulette, so
what about some roulette at the club down the road? And
how about some blue comedians and strip tease in the
clubs? After all, if that old high-class lot could be free-and-
easy about sex, then what about the workers? So just as
the grim tradition of semi-starvation and heroic strikes
came down through old people's talk at the fireside, making
chaps taking 'industrial action' for another ten quid a week
feel heroes too, so perhaps the legend of a hedonistic
Edwardian upper class also came down that way, deciding
how that extra ten quid a week should be spent. But try to
imitate that stuffy old middle-class? No bloody fear!

Lolly and Hard Cash

NO DOUBT THERE are many reasons for my increasing
bewilderment. One of them, I'm certain, has to do with

money—or, to be more accurate, with the way in which I now find myself having to live with two kinds of money. One of them we might call *Lolly,* and the other *Hard Cash.* They seem to belong to two different worlds, and this makes everything difficult for me, sapping my confidence and any lingering sense of security. It's as if I had to keep stepping out of Barclays Bank into the Arabian Nights. At the earning or receiving end, with an entrance that appears to get narrower and narrower, I am of course still in the world of Hard Cash. If we are not writing film scripts or living in Switzerland, we writers are all very much worse off than we used to be. We are all still on the Hard Cash basis and it is getting harder and harder. My various publishers are very decent fellows but it doesn't occur to them to say to one another, 'What about taking old J.B. into the Lolly?'

However, when we are living quietly down here in the country, though the bills may creep up every month, we know roughly where we are. Hard Cash may have to be stretched but we are still living in its familiar world, the one in which we receive our pay. Barclays Bank hasn't vanished. A pound note is still more or less a pound note, and not small change. We have not been whisked away to the Arabian Nights or the Petroleum Club, Dallas, Texas. Cautious cheques arrive from time to time, but neither rail or road services deliver whacking great parcels of tenners and fivers, as they must do in Lollyland. But we haven't to go very far before we realize that we are expected to bring Lolly with us and not our share of Hard Cash. The larger hotels in provincial cities now appear to be Lolly outposts. Gone for ever are the days when they offered you, at a modest price, cut off the joint and two veg or steak and kidney pud. They try to look and behave as if

Michelin had just awarded them a third star. Vast menus are brought to you in the bar, which probably has a fancy name that adds 5p to the cost of each drink. There is much talk of chefs and their Specialities, as if the kitchens were crammed with Cordon Bleu high bonnets. Everything is rather bogus except the bills, which, if you are on a Hard Cash earning basis, are a dreadful reality.

But of course it is London that best represents this world of different money, the lovely Lolly that must be delivered to some people in bales. Even while preparing to travel the ninety miles there, Lolly takes over at the ticket office, so that I seem to be booking first-class sleepers to Inverness. At the other end we might be arriving at a boom town in a gold rush, or celebrating a big win on the football pools or the death of a rich aunt, or, at the lowest estimate, have been turned into drunken sailors. Any Hard Cash earner, unwilling to offer dud cheques, wonders if he ought not to stay indoors, opening tins of baked beans. Surely all the other people can't be property developers or P.R.O. men with vast expense accounts! To begin with, you suddenly find the rent of your flat is about to be doubled. You try one familiar restaurant after another, only to discover that two thin slices of roast beef (vegetables extra) cost £2.75 and that a modest dinner for two, without cocktails, cigars and liqueur brandies, invites a bill of £12. God knows what happens to chaps who really want 'to go on the town' and try the various night clubs, which is something I wouldn't want to do even at somebody else's expense! They must be ready to scatter fivers like confetti. And now what I want to know is this. How do you move from the narrow Hard Cash end, where I seem to be fixed, to the broad free Lolly end, with its private printing machine turning out tenners? How do I exchange money to earn into money to burn? And now do you understand my increasing bewilderment?

Higher Education

MY FATHER WAS a schoolmaster—and a very enthusiastic schoolmaster too, often embarrassing his family by attempting to educate anybody who shared the same railway carriage on our way to the seaside. Moreover, some of his friends were enthusiastic schoolmasters too, with the result that the trials and final marvels of Education were discussed for hours on end, week after week, year after year. And though I had a taste for adult conversation when I was a boy, with a particular relish for heated political argument, I felt there was altogether too much talk about Education. And there still is. I have been thinking about the men I know best, all admired friends, and considering them in terms of Education and Higher Education. And now I have made a curious discovery. These men can be roughly divided into two quite different groups. Either they had a lot of Education, as dazzlingly High as you can go, or they had hardly any at all, achieving well-stored minds by doing the storing themselves. And certainly nobody meeting any members of this second group, the self-educated, would want to make notes for a speech on behalf of the under-privileged. If these forthright men have ever felt they had been under privileged, they have never complained to me about it. On the other hand, one of my oldest friends, who could pick scholarships, Exhibitions, prizes, like ripe pears off the tree, always says, 'I happened to have a very good memory, that's all. And I think most of it was a waste of time.' And I seem to remember that our friend Henry Morris, the creator of the Cambridge Village Colleges and a great character, always maintained that too much was made of what he liked to call 'discourse'. And though, like Henry, a bookish type myself, I have always agreed with him.

Overgrown lads, who can't bother about stuff out of books and hate sitting at those desks, who make a nuisance of themselves out of boredom and a sense of frustration, should be sent straight out of school to some form of apprenticeship, working with grown men who will stand no nonsense from them. (Though ten to one there wouldn't be any.) As for a real apprenticeship to a craft, it is of course an Education itself. I have yet to meet a genuine craftsman who seemed to me *a silly man*. He may be weak on the 'discourse' side, but what he knows he knows thoroughly. He may be said to have explored reality, and he is probably very shrewd in his attitude towards the reality he knows. And this will prevent him from being a fool. I doubt if we can say as much for Higher Education in general, which I suspect sometimes of organizing post-graduate courses in silliness. (Think of some of those sociological antics!) But I can't discover in myself any prejudice against universities: I was up at one and have visited scores of them, in many different countries. I feel they do more good than harm. Yet at the same time I never remember caring a damn whether anybody I met had been or hadn't been to a university.

Show-Biz

I LOVE TALENT. I am ready to raise a cheer whenever and wherever I see talent clearly shining. We are not on the whole a pleasant species. Too much of our behaviour, both in public and private, is contemptible. We infect ourselves with senseless prejudices and passions. Our general conduct probably compares unfavourably with that of chest-thumping gorillas and nitpicking chimpanzees. But there is talent among us, bringing lustre to our dark swarming mass, busy covering and ruining the planet. So we do well to continue applauding the talented. Nevertheless, I detest the business—now the very big business—organizing entertainment and exploiting talent—in short, *Showbiz*. Increasingly it does far more harm than good. It exists not to heighten and enrich entertainment, not to provide the finest talent with wonderful opportunities, but simply for money and power. Somewhere behind its de-luxe suites, its telex services, its acres of mahogany, its champagne and caviare and eight-inch Havanas, is the old fairground showman, promising anything from mermaids to wild men of Borneo to pack 'em in while 'Just commencing!'

I believe Showbiz to be the enemy and not the friend of genuine talent. It is apt to ruin great talent while it inflates and shockingly over-estimates very small and dubious talent. Thanks to Showbiz and its deals and busy publicity men and its almost hypnotic influence on the mass media, many of the most highly-paid performers in the world are men and women who have in fact very little talent, and, like TV regulars, are just well-known for being well-known. On the other hand, poor Tony Hancock, who had great

talent, was neurotically divided and self destructive because
for ever at work in his unconscious was a contempt for, then
a growing hatred of, Showbiz. It has contrived a vast idiots'
dreamland of money and fame, where everybody and everything are all glitter and glamour. And—alas, alas!—the
contrivers of this fake fairyland have entirely conquered TV.
So we have these programmes that are one-fifth talent
and four-fifths Showbiz. We have also more and more of
these Showbiz 'chat programmes', which Elaine May and
Mike Nichols burlesqued so savagely years ago that you
wonder how the nonsense could ever have survived. But
then there are programme planners half out of their minds
with Showbizery.

Fashion

READING ABOUT SOME people's major prejudices, I broke
off—I am a great breaker-off these days—to ask myself
what my own prejudices were. One of them, I concluded,
was a thorough dislike of fashion and of people dominated
by it. If this suggests clothes, though they weren't in the
forefront of my mind, I will deal with them briefly, just to
get them out of the way. Over sixty years ago I was giving
some close attention to what I wore and what I might
possibly afford to buy (not much), and there were occasions,
when I was wearing my light grey pegtop trousers and a
floppy bowtie, when I looked as if I were about to join the
chorus in the second act of *La Bohème*. But now that I am

an old square, I dress like an old square.

The other day, some fashion house—God knows why! sent me a lot of coloured photographs of models, both sexes, wearing its latest creations. And I wondered why all these models had to look so fierce. The young men suggested they had either just deserted from the Foreign Legion or were about to sell fifty fighter-bombers to Peking. Moreover, the girls, who used to try to look seductive, were also a bunch of tough guys. There they were, standing with booted legs wide apart, their eyes narrowed, their mouths pulled down and chins out, as if ready to take whips and chains into a concentration camp. I am sure fashion is at work here, but at what work I hate to think.

More and more I dislike and am deeply suspicious of the increasingly desperate desire to follow fashion in speech and manner, food and drink, decoration and furnishing, books and pictures and plays and films. So many people have to be *IN* and never *OUT*. Even the arts must now keep up with hats and skirts and boots. Painters and writers, play or film directors, emerge from darkness to blink under the concentrated spotlights and then, after taking their turn on a TV arts programme, seem to vanish before us old country folk have any chance to decide if they are any good or not. Sometimes I feel as if I am staring at a merry-go-round driven by jet engines. So what is happening? Have too many people fallen under the spell of passing-time, the uni-dimensional time that is hurrying us (they believe) towards extinction? Are they unconsciously accelerating it? Is that why anything a few years old is out-of-date? We might be existing as cells in some vast organism stricken with a fatal disease in its final terrifying stages.

No Hero-Worship

AT NO TIME of life, barring childhood, have I ever had a hero, one to adore and to follow without further thought. I may be told that this is the result of a narcissistic conceit: I am my own hero. Such an interpretation would not make me angry. There may be something in it. Yet I cannot help feeling that this lack of hero-worship, as distinct from warm admiration, has more to do with a certain strong strain in me of humorous realism, if only because an appreciation of comedy and absurdity prevents admiration from blowing itself up into hero-worship.

Touch of Frost

WHEN I FIRST arrived in Moscow, in the autumn of 1945, I shared a corner one evening with Eisenstein, the famous film director, who could speak English. He was having to be very cagey at that time, and one of the things he muttered, meaning what he said and not trying to flatter me, was that I ought to stay there and teach Soviet dramatists how to write plays. Rather to his surprise, I said that their weaknesses were not the result of any lack of talent, but that they suffered from having been given too much. Under the same circumstances, I added, I would probably have made the same mistakes. To begin with, they had large audiences ready to sit cosily in the theatre for hours and hours, not anxious to go home after about a hundred-and-fifty minutes. If they asked for very large casts, so much the better. They could have as many elaborate sets as they wanted. Probably there was an excellent permanent orchestra at their disposal. So long as their themes kept to the Party line, it was all money for jam. And jam was what came out of it, instead of the good bitter marmalade we produced after being compelled to compress, to save salaries by omitting all unnecessary characters, to use the bare minimum of scenery and effects. In short, the limitations imposed upon us improved our work.

Now I am a whole-hearted believer in spreading the arts around. A lot of people won't want them, but everywhere there will be some people, all ages, 'naturals' I like to call them, to whom the discovery of these arts will be like finding water in the desert. And if this spreading around costs millions, then let it cost millions. It is public money well spent, which is more than can be said about a great deal of public money. On the other hand, I feel that no public money should be spent encouraging vaguely promising young people to become full-time professional artists. It can lead to bitter disappointment, years of misery. Certainly it can be spent discovering how promising their promise is—for example, subsidizing a publisher to print their poems, a little theatre company to try out their plays, a local gallery to exhibit their pictures. But the young people themselves should be given no direct subsidies. They may welcome and enjoy easy money as most of us are ready to do, but what they want still more is a chance to show the public their work and then to begin earning money. It is one thing to want to give everybody a chance;

it is quite another thing to accept and then enlarge upon Gray's *Some mute inglorious Milton here may rest.* I don't believe in this fellow. If he was mute, then he was no Milton. The whole point about Milton is that he was anything but mute. No glory was going to be laid on for him; he talked and wrote himself into it. I don't say there ought to be quite as much discouragement as there was in the West Riding when I grew up there. Its folk had a genius for it. They could invest a word like *writing* with a dreadful irony and mockery you had to face like a January east wind. Nevertheless, I can't help feeling that the arts are like fruit, all the better when ripe because their trees have known a frost or two.

Full Moon

DURING THE LAST few days, nearly all important public conferences appear to have failed. Moreover, both outside and inside this house, almost everything that could go wrong has gone wrong. And this has been the time of the full moon. Now many ancient superstitions have warned us against the full moon. But who cares about them? We look to science, not old wives' tales. But science, which is rapidly catching up with ancient superstitions, is now telling us that the magnetic influence of the full moon is no longer to be despised, for it may have a very considerable effect upon us and our fortunes. Possibly from now on when moonshine is at its brightest, we ought to keep quiet, be watchful, and behave cautiously. And perhaps we ought not to dismiss anything as 'mere moonshine.'

Progress in the Theatre

IT MAY BE true, as younger directors tell us, that by abolishing the prosceniums and their curtains, by using a stage projecting well into the audience, productions can be both more intimate and more economical. But it should be recognized that a good deal has been lost. (The perfect theatre would be able to use the projecting open stage and, when necessary, the proscenium and curtain.) To begin with, there is something unsatisfactory, to my mind, about going into a theatre and having to look at ghostly tables and chairs, rocks and trees, there on the darkened open stage. Again, there is a loss of dramatic effect at the end of each act when no curtain is being used. The descent of the curtain, all the time I was writing plays, was no mere mechanical process, any more than the acting and lighting were. We writers, if we knew our business, indicated the *Curtain* speed we wanted, ranging from a Very Slow, creeping down and almost like a sigh to end the scene, to a *Fast Curtain*, like a brutal shout at such goings-on; and if we had any sense we were on hand when these various *Curtains* were rehearsed. Perhaps more important still is the loss of that magic which belonged to the curtain, raised

to give you your first sight of the other world of the play,
lowered to return you to your own world.

Moreover, when the open curtainless stage arrived, the
footlights had to go. These, called 'floats' in Britain and
'foots' in America, worked notable magic. (I seem to be
writing now for the young.) They came up as the house
lights went down, illuminating the lower folds of the
curtain, as if a sunlight we had never quite known were
arriving in this other world. Again they fought the drastic
top-lighting that threatens actresses' good looks. Finally,
we not only varied the colours of the 'floats' but also
planted among them tiny 'baby spots' that would stealthily
illuminate a little table or a single chair. And now at a
time when provincial theatres may be turned into bingo
halls, surely there is something to be said for restoring
some of the old magic? We don't have to be disenchanted
out of everything.

A Little Advice

LET US SUPPOSE that in *The School for Scandal*, Sheridan
had decided that Sir Peter Teazle had called in two ruffians
who beat up Lady Teazle so that she fell, bleeding and
senseless. Or, that in *Pride and Prejudice*, Mr Bennet, un-
able to endure Mr Collins any longer, had knocked his
brains out with a paperweight. Neither the play nor the
novel would be a classic but only a curiosity, known to a

few scholars. But what am I doing now, just being silly? Not at all. I am offering a little advice to new playwrights and novelists. If they are creating plays and novels about violence and crime, well and good. But if they are writing plays and novels, for example, that are concerned with personal relationships, telling us why Lucy and Joe disagree, why Henry and his father misunderstand each other, they must avoid scenes so violent that we want to scream for a doctor and the police. Once we are shot into this atmosphere, the subtleties of personal relationships, psychological lights and shadows, diminish and probably disappear. I admit that men of genius, working on a great scale, have successfully taken us from one atmosphere into another. But, still advising new playwrights and novelists, I would suggest they assume they are not men of genius, about to work on a great scale. Even the geniuses were nearly always cautious at first.

Drinking Time

DRINK, IT USED to be said, is the shortest way out of Manchester. This is not of course a topical saying. It goes back to the time when drink was very cheap and Manchester was very dark and grim. All that was in another world. I am not suggesting we should return to it. Even so, I think if I were running the country I would bring down the price of drink with the possible exception of champagne and those sweet liqueurs, more likely to be made by industrial chemists than by patient old monks. When a government and the industrial system it admires create between them more and more worries and pressures, it seems to me a mean trick to pile more and more duty on drink and tobacco, which help men to feel easier in their minds and to exchange confidences. Probably it is this trick that explains a certain sourness in our society, together with a desire to grab more money even if it means a loss of honour and decency.

When I first arrived in London in the early 1920s I was introduced to a lot of hard drinking, in and around Fleet Street. The talk was probably the best I have ever heard, but it was nourished by round after round of 'doubles.' The hardest drinkers kept to whisky, and I remember a very influential man of letters, staying with me, drinking a whole bottle *before lunch*. Oddly enough, these men neither neglected their work (though they ought to have been writing books instead of articles and reviews) nor died young; and I cannot remember one of them ever being quarrelsome and bellicose. And unlike the next generation of literary critics, they were never pompous, priggish and arrogant. They floated gently from office to pub to desk to book to pub again.

There was even harder and more dangerous drinking, I found, in America under Prohibition. This was the only time I have drunk whisky and gin—very strong and dubious—in the middle of the morning. I would call, let us say, about ten-thirty on a publisher or editor, and he would immediately announce that he had 'something very special, just off the boat' and to refuse a drink or two would have been insulting. A day begun like that could end at two in the morning, in a speakeasy owned by gangsters. As bad mistakes that went on and on, Prohibition and Vietnam get the prizes.

Recently I have read some rather ominous statements by medical men equating hard drinking—incidentally, not one of my weaknesses—with alcoholism. Both may want to blur reality, but one is an expensive and stupid habit, the other a disease. Hard drinkers enjoy booze; alcoholics hate it but must have it. My wife, an authority on the distant past, tells me that men just emerging from the mists of lost time were already busy fermenting intoxicating drink. No doubt we abuse our liberty to take in alcohol. But then we abuse our liberty to set cars in motion. In fact, we abuse our liberty, being imperfect creatures. But not so many people would want to blur reality with drink, boozing not out of sociability but out of desperation, if the reality we have created were less forbidding.

My advice now, coming out of long experience, is addressed to young men. Never never drink hard when you are filled with self-pity and miserable. Give yourself a job, even if it is only painting some bookshelves. Unless there is some hereditary taint, you will never become an alcoholic if you do no drinking until you have done your day's work. If you have to prime yourself to get the work done, sooner or later you will be in bad trouble. Two fine actors I have known were in the sharpest contrast here. One of them, still in magnificent form, never takes a drink until the final curtain is down, and then, his work well done, he will pour out gin as if it were water. The other needed a whole bottle of gin just to get through a performance, and after many a disaster he died. Strong drink is not a medicine: it is a bonus, a spirit to lift our spirit a little but never to quench it.

Do They Overdo It?

THOUGH THE WOMAN I live with in sweet harmony is certainly an exception, I will risk this generalization. It seems to me that most women with brilliant academic records, whether in the arts or sciences, women who become fairly well-known 'intellectuals', work harder than men at suppressing the irrational and instinctive sides of themselves. Determined to remove themselves as far as possible from the illogical and intuitive feminine creature accepted in masculine legends and popular opinion, they have coldly set to work to overdo their intellectuality. So they become too sceptical of the impulsive and intuitive in human nature; they are altogether too rational; and jeopardize their happiness by being too defiant of their unconscious. But I must declare again that this is not true of the woman I know best.

Malaise

IN JUNE 1913 I sailed on a 'butter boat' from Goole to Copenhagen. The second day out, the captain, friendly up to that time, ordered me off the bridge for talking Socialism at him. (I was eighteen years of age and probably insufferable.) I can't remember what I said but I can imagine it, and I would be willing to bet money that every argument I used I could no longer sustain now. Ten to one I told the purpling skipper that everything would be different as soon as men were no longer working for 'the bosses' but for their fellow citizens. Look at the Post Office! (A very familiar gambit then.) Why, once the state had taken over the mines, the railways, steel, textiles, shipping lines that carried butter from Copenhagen, there would be no more bitter disputes, strikes, picketing, ugly scenes! In a few years everybody would be knocking off about three o'clock, ready for folk dancing, wood-carving, lectures on William Morris.

Well, I don't have to rub it in. We live and learn. But do we? I can't help wondering if most economists and politicians are any more realistic and perceptive than I was in 1913, straight out of the egg and just cackling. It seems to be generally agreed that we in England are now suffering from a peculiar malaise. Sometimes I think it all began when Prime Minister Macmillan told us we had never had it so good. (A phrase unwisely chosen.) Advertising on the telly and in the colour mags took over. You had only to buy something to win an entrance into the Good Life, except of course that you had to buy something else to be really there. Hire purchase was flashed on and off like traffic signals. Soon there was more talk and writing about money than I had heard or read before in a long lifetime. We were halfway into America at a time when so many decent Americans were halfway out. Cars were bought by the mile to enjoy carbon-monoxide weekends. There were lads who spent more on clothes in a month than I do in a year. The male-toilet-trade rose to dizzy intoxicating heights. Coach parties to the sexiest plays roared off every week night. New clubs for the workers might have been spawned by

Las Vegas. There were travel agencies down every other street. O-ho – the Good Life!

But more and more money was needed, the Good Life never offering something for nothing as the stuffy old-fashioned things often did. And we were not doing so well. Though Good Lifers to a man—and with the women and children making their demands too—when it came to racing towards the big money we tended to loiter and sulk and turn awkward. Some deep instinctive *very English* feeling in us would not allow us to try hard enough. We wanted the Good Life but not at any price. And here is the notorious malaise, with all its bloody-minded symptoms. We are a people sorely divided in both our public and private worlds, not able to ask ourselves *what we really want*. If you see a political-economic problem here, then go ahead and start solving it. But I don't. Finally, if you tell me I have said all this before, you are quite right. I propose to go on saying it, with some variations, until some politicians, economists, social critics, see what I mean or I am compelled, once and for all, to shut up.

Praise—For Once

A BRIEF THANKSGIVING. The other night, after switching on the TV set quite casually, I thought about my father, who died in 1924. The set had just shown me a flight of birds against a tropical background, in colour that wasn't harsh or too bright and could have come out of a good painter's palette. My father, one of the old brigade of nature-lovers, returned to my mind because I thought how this picture of the birds, so conveniently and magically delivered, would have delighted him. What a difference this kind of TV would have made to his last months, when he was still moving around but was in fact a dying man! How deeply I regretted he had never had the chance to sit at home and see America, Asia, Africa, their flowers, their trees, their birds, filling and colouring the screen. I know all about the foolishness and fuss of TV, and the way in which some of its rubbish captures the public mind. But for once I propose to be thankful for it, to salute the scientists and technologists who made it possible. And made other things possible too.

Ours is a great age of reproduction and recording, catering lavishly for both eye and ear. It is as if we realized that our civilization, beginning at the Renaissance, might be now coming to an end. It may be our task to leave behind, on such a scale that some of it must endure, an account of what our centuries have achieved in the arts. And for my part, I have taken great delight in these reproductions and records. The older I get, the more I feel I owe them. There are some art critics and historians, I know, who despise or furiously condemn all attempts at reproducing great paintings: we must either go and see the pictures themselves or forget about them. This seems to me pedantic, snobbish and unimaginative. More than once I have reached a keener and deeper appreciation of a master's work, after brooding over reproductions of it in solitude, than I have by attending crowded exhibitions of it, with concentration ruined by the presence of so many other people. After all, most of us don't have galleries and museums specially opened for us.

As for music, for anybody possessing a good stereo record-player, its recordings can be a constant joy. We may miss the excitement of an actual concert—and up to the last few years I attended many concerts and even organized a series of them to please my neighbours—yet the music is there, often better heard, ready to tune itself to any mood. I shall be told, ten to one not pleasantly, that this kind of thing costs money. And indeed I know it does, but even so there are gramophone societies to be joined, and there is always the radio. Books I shall ignore, because with them the gains and losses cancel out. But I hasten to offer thanks to astronomers, who with larger and larger telescopes and with radio astronomy, have introduced us to a universe of ever-increasing size and complexity. Then again, the space probes have brought us new marvels. Though I cannot understand the science, I glow with curiosity and wonder, I don't shrink from the thought of billions of gigantic suns, the illimitable chasms of space, even those *black holes* where light itself perishes: I delight in it all. But this is chiefly because I believe we are looking at something we can't really comprehend, just as the cells in our bodies can't comprehend us, and I also believe that *it is all alive*. As we must try to be.

Not Happy on the Day

EVER SINCE ABOUT 1904 I have been disappointing my loved ones on Christmas Day. They have wanted me to be happy and I have never looked and behaved as if I were feeling happy. The trouble is, I can never feel happy when I am *expected* to feel happy. It's not that I am really a miserable fellow. On a bitter day in February or a sultry one in August, I might easily be discovered almost radiant with high spirits, nearly a fountain of joy: it would do your heart good to be near me. But something in me resists the *calendar expectation* of happiness. *Merry Christmas yourself!*—it mutters as it shapes a ghastly grin.

Brown Eggs

LET US MAKE a modest start—as I do four mornings out of five—with eggs. Now here in England most of us, all ages, prefer brown eggs to white eggs. In America, brown eggs are despised, sold off cheaply, perhaps sometimes thrown away. Can any sense be made out of this queer difference in taste? I believe it can. But will it take us anywhere? Yes, I believe it will. Not only that—behavioral sciences, please note—it will move us almost at once from the visible world of white eggs and brown eggs into the vast invisible realm where our lives are shaped.

We English prefer brown eggs because they seem to us to have a more reliable look of rusticity. They are closer to Nature, and appear to promise us a richer and more sustaining interior. A brown egg, we feel, has come to us, magically perhaps, straight out of the ancient pastoral world. Unlike the white egg, it has escaped factory farming, machines and mass production, higher productivity. It belongs to the enduring dream of the English, who ever since the Industrial Revolution have created wretched towns chiefly because they never really accepted urban life, always hoping to move sooner or later into the country. What we English want is to live in the country, with some splendid free-range fowls just down the road, none of your deprived and pallid prisoners of the battery, desperately ridding themselves of smaller and smaller white eggs; and then to enjoy every morning a big brown egg. Any public man in England who does not understand this cannot understand the English, and should retire from public life—into the country.

The Americans, well outside the ghettoes, despise brown eggs just because they do seem closer to Nature. White eggs are much better, especially if they are to be given to precious children, because their very whiteness suggests hygiene and purity, for which Americans have a passion that we English do not share. It is as if Nature, after being taught some hard lessons, had been forced to attempt some progressive hygienic packaging with that white shell.

It is a mistake—and one that is all too common—to accuse Americans of being 'materialistic'. They are far less so than, for example, the Chinese and the French, the best cooks in the world. The weakness of American civilization, and perhaps the chief reason why it creates so much discontent, is that it is so curiously abstract. It is a bloodless extrapolation of a satisfying life. For all those thick steaks and gammon rashers, all that scotch and bourbon, a melancholy enchantment seems to turn it into statistics and mere images of good living. You dine off the advertiser's 'sizzling' and not the meat of the steak. Sex is discovered in manuals and not in bed. And as soon as guaranteed egg-substitute has been packaged and marketed, from a huge factory in New Jersey called 'Old Mother Giles', then real white eggs will be even more sharply despised than brown eggs are now.

* * * * * * * *

NOTE. I have included this piece for a special reason. It opened a series of short pieces I wrote for *The New Statesman*, under the general title of *The Uneasy Chair*. Though never intended to be taken solemnly, it was picked up by important newspapers on both sides of the Atlantic. Then within a few hours I was bombarded by cables and long-distance phone calls. Invitations to reply to criticism in writing or on TV and radio came pouring in. I believe a new young writer could have almost based a career on these brown and white eggs. Dismissing it as a lot of silly fuss, just a storm in an eggcup, I replied to nobody, took no notice of anybody, and went on with my work. But I would have welcomed all the money that was wasted on those cables and long-distance phone calls.

Public Attention

AS FAR AS I can remember, I have never sought for personal publicity and have often taken great care to avoid it. I mention this to dismiss any notion of 'sour grapes' in what I am about to declare. The almost instant fame of regular TV performers—interviewers, programme 'anchor men', announcers—does this country more harm than good. There is nothing wrong with these chaps; they do their work as well as it can be done; but there is no sensible reason why they should be put upon pedestals. Wide and varied though it may appear to be, the amount of public attention is limited. If one set of people are claiming too much of it, then other men and women, who may have far more to offer the community, are not receiving their share of it. Politics, the arts and sciences begin to suffer from a lack of attention. A certain silliness begins to invade the public mind. There is a surfeit of being 'well-known for being well-known', of reputations blown up like so many bladders, of celebrities who have little or nothing to celebrate. There is no sustenance for a society here: it is feeding itself on the wind.

The Giant Teas

NOW AND AGAIN I keep recalling certain occasions in my boyhood. I would be sitting alone at a very large table, which offered me the ruins, still luscious, of a gigantic high tea. These occasions ranged from a domestic whist drive—four tables, with prizes, top to booby—to a family funeral, which always demanded a splendid high tea; and for various reasons all of them looking good to me, I was allowed to eat alone when everybody else had finished and had gone into the next room, either to play whist or tell tales of the departed. These high teas had everything, from roast pork and noble 'stand pies' to trifles, jellies, tarts, all manner of rich cakes, and might have been a feast out of the Arabian Nights. The fact that sixteen people had already gorged away at it didn't worry me at all, for there was always plenty of everything left, nobody to tell me what to eat and how to eat it, and I might have been one of the decadent Roman emperors sitting there, master of all I saw and already licking my lips. No doubt I was a greedy lad. (Now I look a greedy old man, though in fact I am not.) Remembering such moments, I have a notion that neither my five children nor their children, my fifteen grandchildren, can recall anything like them. It is not only that the vast high teas have vanished, together with all their variety of enticements. I think the greediness has gone too, and perhaps only those of us who were born in Victoria's reign ever really knew it. My family are robust eaters but I cannot believe any one of them has ever known the gluttonous wonder and joy of those occasions, when I sat there, alone, surveying a little continent of savoury and sweet delights, with nobody to say 'Surely you've had enough!'

The Letters—Oh, The Letters!

THAT MUST BE taken as a mournful cry. One of the drawers in my desk was so full of letters, the kind I intended to keep, that I could no longer open it properly. So I pulled out the nearest letters and then worked my way through all of them, going back about ten years. There were letters from loving friends, admiring colleagues, and some last words from old friends now dead and gone. There were business notes about plans that never worked out or triumphantly succeeded. But no matter what they were, they moved me deeper and deeper into a swamp of melancholy. There might be moments of grief, for the dead friends, or flashes of gratitude for some sentences of deep understanding, but what had happened before now happened again: the mists gathered over the swamp and I went backing further and further into it. (Perhaps I ought not to bother with this, for I gather that the experience is fairly common.) The name of the evil magician who works this spell, wiping out loving interest, thanks or grief, is *Futility*. After the first hour or two, trying to decide which letters should still be kept, he begins whispering, 'Ten years, eh? *Ten years! So what?*' And I have no reply ready for him. I cannot even wonder stoutly if there is some reality into which I have never penetrated, some other world where he would never be allowed even one whisper. And now I understand why, year after year, I put off going through the letters until the drawer can hardly be opened.

Rembrandt

IN NOVEMBER 1969 I wrote an account of a visit I paid to the great Rembrandt Exhibition in Amsterdam, an account that appeared in the *New Statesman*. The concluding paragraphs on Rembrandt himself seem to me worth reprinting here because several correspondents, all mature sensible men, wrote to say that this was the kind of art criticism they understood and enjoyed. So here goes.

What wing home to me like great tame eagles are Rembrandt's later self-portraits. I don't mean they look like eagles, but then that *Self-Portrait as the Apostle Paul*, which lives in the Rijksmuseum, looks as much like the Apostle Paul as I do. It is just Rembrandt, getting on and wondering how things will turn out, wearing a turban and holding a few apostle props. But to say *just Rembrandt* is nonsense; it dims and diminishes the splendour of these later self-portraits, which began to fascinate me when I was much younger than I am now. I have contrived to live twelve years longer than Rembrandt did, but that is a combination of antibiotics and a want of that greatness of spirit which can wear a man out. Roughly speaking we can be said to be of an age, though I am ready to allow that the great painter even now is really a few years older than I am, more thoroughly steeped in experience. But anyhow, there we are, two old men, face to face. And I find more and more in him, the oftener and longer I look.

These self-portraits give me what I want from art. They offer me two things that foolish people imagine are never found together. The first is deliberate and unflinching realism. But let us be careful here. True realism must be coolly objective, an acceptance and delineation of life as it really is. It must not be confused, as it is all too often, with the darkening and distortion that come from self-tormenting minds. Too many sick travesties, monstrous little worlds made by despair out of clay and wormwood, are offered to us as the newest and bravest realism. We might as well accept no reports upon life that do not reach us from a lunatic asylum. There are fashionable critics who have wandered so long in half-ruined minds that they are lost to the common scene.

There is nothing of this in Rembrandt's later self-portraits. He paints what the glass shows him. He no longer looks young and confident and is not going to pretend he is weathering wonderfully. The nose is more bulbous than ever; cheeks are sagging; there are telltale lines and shadows everywhere; this is no map of euphoria. But neither is it one of the caricatures that subjectivity and self-disgust produce together. It is a face that might have known some boozy late nights and lust for women, and much else that a man might be glad to forget, but he does not cheat by offering us an ageing satyr or a dribbling sot, which would only be a further kind of self-indulgence. He paints what is there and not what in weaker moments he thinks ought to be there. He accepts without distortion the honest truth. And this is what I call realism, and it is rare.

But there is something else, the second of the two things I mentioned above. It is not as obvious as the realism. To discover it we need to spend some time alone with these self-portraits, to brood and meditate upon them, perhaps to lose ourselves in them. When we do this, it seems to me that while Rembrandt shows us his everyday self we feel he is also looking through us and beyond us. He is telling us very quietly that life is a mystery. When he put down his brushes for the last time, clever men were just beginning to put together—a spring here, a cogwheel there—that clockwork universe in which the more enlightened persons of the eighteenth century would find themselves. But

Rembrandt is peering the other way. I said of Shakespeare once: "He recognizes that life is a mystery, that man and Nature are symbolic representations, that we can feel if not think our way through our sense of beauty and goodness, to a reality behind appearances, as the lives of the dramatist and players are in a deeper reality behind the shows of the playhouse."

Rembrandt is another member of that noble rare company. He gives us honest realism and then something beyond it, a glimpse of a deeper reality. Consider how in painting after painting the scene emerges from darkness, to be so truthfully and wonderfully illuminated, and then fades into darkness again, like the consciousness our psyche has so newly achieved. And then, to crown it all, to give us a sign before he vanishes, that last look he offers us in the late self-portraits! To be reminded again of what a great artist can do, of how an art, balanced between extraversion and introversion, can show us ordinary sane reality and then lead us beyond it, increasing our sense of wonder and awe— wasn't this worth a hasty trip abroad, a squandering of guilders, all that coping with gaggles of schoolgirls? It was indeed. The exhibition closes on the 30th of this month.

Sensuality! Cold and Warm

IF WE ARE to have an after-life, going through the grave like a door, it has been generally agreed that we shall have to do without the body. Not an ounce of flesh, a drop of blood, will go with us. This has encouraged a host of men, down the centuries, to ignore or condemn all bodily pleasures, mortifying the senses as a kind of insurance for this next life. Why depend upon the body if soon we must do without it? The sensuality we enjoy today may sooner or later be so much bitter frustration.

Clearly I can't prove this attitude of mind to be wrong, not having tried the after-life. Even so, I think it is wrong because it lacks discrimination. I believe there are two kinds of sensuality. (And I am not afraid of using the pejorative term.) One might be imagined as cold and heavy, the other as light and warm. The ascetic or grim puritan, busy subduing the flesh in preparation for the next life, understands the first kind, the cold and heavy, in exile after the grave; but is temperamentally incapable of appreciating this other sensuality that is light and warm. Now this way of enjoying what flesh and blood offer us, I feel, can survive the death of the body. It is not simply an affair of nerve endings and the 'limbic' portion of the brain. There is in it soul or spirit or whatever one chooses to call the non-material element. It is also a sensuality that is not entirely divorced from poetry and ideas.

I had no sooner written the above when I suddenly remembered myself in the Paris of 1946, when I had gone to attend the first Unesco Conference. I was staying at the luxurious George V hotel, and after the austerities of Britain the food at dinner seemed wonderful. But after a night or two I found I could not enjoy these dinners, simply because there I was, alone, luxuriously stuffing myself. This marks, I feel, the difference between the two kinds of sensuality. A cold heavy sensualist, gobbling away without any interruption, would have been quite happy. But it simply wasn't good enough for the light warm sensualist, for the sensuality that has not detached itself from imagination, the poetry of life, the spirit, and so may outlast the death of the body.

Better Dead

THE PEOPLE WHO pretend that dying is rather like strolling into the next room always leave me unconvinced. Death, like birth, must be a tremendous event. But while the thought of it is constantly with me—and I cannot take it lightly—it does not reduce me to fits of fear and trembling. On the other hand, I am really frightened of our doctors. Not all of them of course, but those who believe it is their duty to preserve life at all costs, to keep you going if necessary as a vegetable, all dignity and decency gone. I believe this to be all wrong, and I fancy that nine people out of ten would agree with me. We are not machines, to be endlessly tinkered with so long as something works, but persons, and as soon as we can no longer be regarded as persons, in constant communication with those who love us, we should be allowed to die as soon as possible. We do not enter hospitals as so much material for research, and any idea that we do represents contemporary science in its dehumanizing phase, with curiosity driving out natural piety.

A Dream

WHILE I DREAM as much as ever, the dreams vanish on
my waking and I cannot remember any part of them. And I
take this to mean that such dreams have nothing of any
importance to say to me. It is the dreams that insist upon
being remembered, often in sharp detail, that have something important to say, even though their message may be
hard to interpret. The last dream of this rare sort—rare at
least to me nowadays—came some months after the death
of one of my oldest friends, whom I will call T.D. It began
by my finding myself alone in a large sitting-room, not in
my own house. A number of people came in, chattering
away, and then I noticed that my friend T.D. had also
entered but was hanging back in a diffident fashion, quite
unlike his usual style. This puzzled me until I remembered
that he was dead. (I assumed that the other people, who did
not interest me, were not dead.) I went across to my friend,
who was still hanging back, put a hand on his shoulder and
said, 'I'm very very glad to see you here, T.' Then I woke
up, still aware of the rough tweed resisting the pressure of
my hand on his shoulder. Now what created this dream?
Freudians can keep quiet about any repressed homosexual
tendencies if only because I could easily prove, if it were
worth while here, that I have long been aware, without any
need of a censor, of any sexual antics in my mind. The
Spiritualists will claim me at once, of course, but I do not
accept their account of our after-life. So what remains,
according to my own beliefs? As I have suggested elsewhere, it seems to me that consciousness is not contained
within passing-time and so survives in some measure the

death of the body. Outside time and bodyless, perhaps feeling confused and inadequate (hence his diffidence), my old friend knew he was still *alive* and badly wanted to tell me so. By some means I do not pretend to understand, this desire-cum-thought reached my unconscious, itself partly timeless, which then staged the dream I have described. I accepted his message by ignoring the other people to welcome him.

No Man of Action

AT VARIOUS TIMES during the last thirty-five years I have disappointed people I liked who had a high opinion of me. The fact is, we were always at cross purposes. Because of something I wrote, and then because I had a deep voice or bristling eyebrows or an apparently masterful presence, they assumed they had in me a man of action, a potential leader. Then they discovered that I wandered away, muttering excuses, to escape this role, which indeed is one that I have never wanted. I knew very well I was not a man of action. I had not the least desire to lead anybody. (Moreover I have always privately detested the routine of political or semi-political movements—the committees, the resolutions, the agendas, the public meetings, the platform palavers.) What I really am is at least no secret: I am—and have been from early youth—*a writer*. It was never any use saying to me, as people so often did: 'You have written it and excited us. Now *DO* something!' To a man of my temperament, vocation and profession, when I have written something I have done what is in me to do. The writing is my contribution. Perhaps some of it might have been a lot better, but the worst of it would be preferable to my leadership or attempts to play the man of action. It has never been a question of moral courage (though no hero, I am not lacking that) nor of a certain physical indolence (though a taint there, perhaps); even if I will admit that I am too easily bored by familiar routines and the tactics of earnest power-seeking types. The point is, I was always far better acquainted with my own character and capacities than all those other people were. But if this should catch the attention of a few eager reformers who were disappointed, let me end by saying that I am sorry.

Idiotic Criticism

IT OUGHT TO be obvious that in any novels and plays worth considering most of the characters are expressing themselves, only a very few indeed serving as the author's mouthpieces. (Sometimes, none at all.) Any decently-taught schoolboy ought to know this. Yet time after time I have found reviewers and critics, writing in serious journals, falling into this silly trap. For example, I remember being bitterly attacked for the opinions of a self-indulgent old clubman I had introduced into the narrative, opinions a

whole world away from my own. I could only conclude
that the critic in question was half out of his mind or was
so anxious to throw something at me that he picked up the
nearest brick that caught his eye. But even if, about then, I
was a tempting target, a critic did not have to make an ass
of himself to prove he was right there—in the movement.

Her Communism

I WAS MEETING after a long interval a woman I had known
and greatly liked for many years, ever since she was a
young girl. She was still quite young when she turned
Communist, and though she may not be a Party member,
she had not rejected her faith in the movement. She knew I
had visited various Communist countries, and hastily told
me, 'Our Communism will be quite different.' I didn't reply,
'Like hell it will!' but the thought crossed my mind. I might
have told her that after a short period of enthusiasm and
high hopes, it would go down the same grim path. Very
soon all opposition or even reasonable criticism would be
ruthlessly silenced and then punished. Boring and idiotic
propaganda would take over the country. Gigantic lies
would come through all the loud speakers. History would
be faked. And nice women like her would either retreat
into a close-mouthed melancholy or turn themselves into
shrieking Marxist-Leninist maenads. Few people are so
terrible as frustrated idealists, who begin to despise or hate

ordinary human nature because it insists upon behaving like ordinary human nature. I dislike large-scale capitalism because it turns itself into a huge swindle. But even so, I would rather be at the mercy of cynical fellows, busy feathering their nests, than find myself the victim of frustrated and finally merciless idealists.

Continuous Telepathy

THAT ENCHANTING MAN, Walter de la Mare, seems to have believed that telepathy is almost continuous and that without some form of telepathic communication we could hardly carry on a satisfactory conversation. This may seem a startling idea, but I am beginning to suspect that it may be true. (The examples, now fairly familiar, of instant communication at a distance, usually concerned with death or some disaster, would be the same thing raised to a higher and more dramatic power by intense emotion. The weakness of controlled or lab experiments is that they not only don't involve such emotion but usually fall below the level of interest of any talk that is more than idle chat.) De la Mare's continuous telepathy could explain something that has always puzzled me. This is the way in which, perhaps after a first brief meeting, when nothing highly personal has been said, we cannot help feeling that a person is sympathetic or antipathetic, is on our side or against us. I realize of course that appearance, voice, manner, may all play their parts, but very often what we have observed does not explain this feeling. It is as if more has been happening during those few minutes than can be taken into ordinary account, and there has been inner as well as outer communication. So de la Mare's belief should not be dismissed too hastily.

Dislike of Ceylon

WHY DO WE like or even love some places we have visited and dislike others? I asked myself this question again when I read today yet another rapturous account of Ceylon. My wife enjoyed our stay in Ceylon; several of our friends are enthusiastic about it; and Mr Arthur Clarke, the deservedly popular writer of science-fiction, prefers to make his home in Colombo when he could live anywhere he chooses. In all this I seem to be the odd man out. Though I didn't tell Mr Clarke so, I wouldn't live in Colombo or anywhere else in Ceylon, not if I were paid £10,000 a year just for doing it. Nor do I believe that I simply added up a number of minor irritations until I had created a feeling of unease deepening into detestation. Ceylon often seemed as beautiful as it was generally supposed to be; we met and were entertained by a number of very pleasant people; we were lodged and boarded in a fairly adequate fashion for a tropical island. Yet I never felt at ease there, as I had done in so many places wildly different from England. If I magnified the minor irritations, always to be expected in distant travel, it was because somewhere deep down below them was a feeling, which refused to leave me, that this island and I could never be on good terms. It was just as if in some previous existence—and I must add at once that I don't believe in previous existences—I had been one of the wretched fellows who had been cruelly tortured in or near Kandy. Ceylon's history is divided between long peaceful stretches of reservoir building and outbursts of appalling violence and cruelty, and it was as if my unconscious was obscurely aware, on a mysterious wavelength, of these abominable outbursts and their orgies of sadism, and some feeling of revulsion seeped through into consciousness. And it is an odd fact that the only happy day (for me) was the one we spent climbing up to Nowara Eliya, where the British, to escape the heat, had created a little mock-English town and a Victorian-Edwardian club where we lunched and found everything at once absurd and delightful. This may prove that behind a façade of progressive liberalism, I am at heart an old-fashioned Imperialist. As far as Ceylon is concerned—less and less a bright star in the East—I think I am. And I cannot help remembering that until a member of the British Colonial Service toiled away to piece it together, the islanders didn't even know their own history.

Chapel

I N T H E E A R L Y years of this century I had to attend Sunday morning service at a nonconformist chapel and Sunday school in the afternoon. Much later, when I was reading widely, I began to explore all manner of religions, though never joining them in their places of worship. But as a boy, sitting in chapel in my best suit, I did no worshipping at all, was visited by no emotion but felt detached from all the proceedings. Our dourest parsons, who followed the nonconformist fashion of long extemporary prayers, always seemed to me to be bent on bullying God. After a few *Beseech Thees* as a mere politeness, they adopted a sterner tone and told Him what they expected from Him and more than hinted He must attend to His work. What might be all right long ago in the Near East, to which we sometimes confusingly returned, would not do for Bradford in 1905. And the hymns, to which I occasionally lent a voice, seemed to me either grim or idiotic.

But this was all on Sunday—known to some of the deacons as *The Sabbath*. Was the building silent throughout the week, puritanically brooding on who might be saved? It certainly was not. The main room of the Sunday School was fairly large and it had a number of useful classrooms. These crackled or hummed with life many a day and most evenings. There were sewing meetings, gymnastic classes for the young men, teas-and-concerts, lantern lectures, conjuring entertainments, and—best of all, the bazaars, which kept people happily busy for weeks and weeks and were then uproarious affairs for three or four nights, during which I promoted myself into being announcer and 'barker' for the various entertainments. At the same time the regular chapelgoers created their own little circles of friends, who invited one another to magnificent high teas (with rum out of 'a little brown jug') and then played whist, always leading their aces, or sang drawing-room ballads—I accom-

panied dozens of them. Nowadays we are asked to listen
to the desperate cries of the lonely. It seems that in our
many-towered cities there are decent people eating their
hearts out with loneliness. I tell you, anybody who regularly
attended Westgate Baptist Chapel, Manningham, Bradford, when I was a boy there, never suffered from this
affliction.

Who Have Been Soaked?

AFTER RUMMAGING AT the back of a cupboard, I found
I had told a correspondent about twenty-seven years ago
that imposing stiff income-and-surtaxes was no way to begin closing the gap between the wealthy, who owned so
much, and the people who owned little or nothing. As I
write this, we are still talking about it now, after twenty-
seven years and so much brave leftish talk about 'soaking
the rich.' But the rich were never soaked except by the
tides around the Bahamas. The soakers rarely reached the
genuine wealthy, who by sheer ownership could have their
money piling up while they drank planter's punches in
Jamaica. It was hard-working successful professional men
and women who were herded every year to the shearers,
people who hardly owned anything except their skill and
capacity to keep on working, who if they ran into ill-health
or bad luck might soon find themselves facing poverty. I
know because I have been one of them, though so far

without the ill-health and bad luck: exploiting nobody, not getting any money for nothing, working hard to produce something and then, so to speak, passing round the hat. Yet for years I have been reading about Thingummy's millions or about young So-and-So being 'well on his way towards his first million.' And we don't even know what these fellows have been up to! But let a young playwright have a lucky year and on the stiff income-and-surtax principle most of his money will be taken away from him; and in a few years he may be back living in a basement on tinned beans. And by this time young So-and-So may have made another million, if he has not settled down in a distant tax haven. I once read somewhere that British taxation was based on equity. I rubbed my eyes.

Danger of Shock Tactics

SOME TIME AGO, in an interview that turned towards the Theatre, I suggested that 'Pubic hair is not an adequate substitute for wit.' I should like now to extend and broaden this critical front. While I happen to believe that intimate sex is within the province of the poet or novelist, who can describe it *from the inside*, the playwright, with his solid bodies on the stage, is outside this province; but this is not the line I want to take here. My point now is that depending upon shock tactics is easy whereas writing a good play is difficult, and that it is tempting to the young playwright to take the easier way. After all, it demands very little skill to show young men masturbating, lesbians romping, copulation in various positions; but writing a satisfactory play, solidly constructed, creating characters that are not lunatics, suggesting life beyond the confines of the stage, all this can demand patience, thought, skill, self-criticism. So it is not prudery that makes me believe that if shock tactics are abandoned, sooner or later we might find we are offered more good plays, widening and deepening our sympathies and not in the titillation business.

Memory

WHENEVER I WENT to Bradford and met people I had known in boyhood and early youth, a curious thing happened. They were people who had remained in Bradford and had led rather dull routine lives. I on my part had done a thousand things and had travelled all over the world. With this difference in mind, they were surprised that I should remember them at all. But as we talked it became clear to me that almost always I could recall far more than they could. It was not that I had been busy remembering these early years—I had probably been deeply immersed in something very different—but that once I had started to challenge my memory, these years were found to be still alive in it, whereas their recollections had been dulled and devitalized by time. Probably we thought about our lives in a different way. They were more or less hypnotized by their immediate situation, what they were when I met them again, while I tended to think of my whole life as one living whole —the 'long body' of Indian thought.

That Small Fish

SOMETIMES I FIND myself thinking, rather wistfully, about Lao Tzu's famous dictum: 'Govern a great nation as you would cook a small fish.' All around me I see something very different, let us say—a number of anxious or angry dwarfs trying to grill a whale.

Listening

I AM A polite man who has long had the reputation of being a rude man. When I say I am a polite man, I don't mean to suggest that I am for ever smiling and have a smooth manner and shower compliments on people. I consider myself polite because when people talk to me I really *listen* and am not just thinking about what I will say next or wondering, at a party, if there is somebody more important I ought to be joining. And this seems to me ample compensation for what may be taken for a brusque manner. Most women are sharply aware of the difference between real listening and considering and a mere polite smiling pretence, and this is why on the whole I get along with them.

The Brain

THIS AFTERNOON I have been reading once again about the marvels of the brain, with its hundred billion neurons or nerve cells, its chemical reactions that may take as little as one-millionth of a second. Clearly this electronic wonder inside my skull is far cleverer than I am. Most of the time it teaches me, I don't teach it. But notice how I am phrasing this, quite unlike most of the brain specialists. Being both 'woolly-minded' and obstinate, I still insist that this is *my brain*: it *isn't me*. And indeed to be 'woolly-minded', I must have a mind; it isn't my brain that is woolly. Furthermore, though without any support as yet from the labs, I believe it will be discovered scientifically, sooner or later, that the brain does not represent a closed system: that somehow it is open-ended, and that, for example, its fantastic memory-banking, far exceeding what is necessary for the life of our species, will be found to have a special significance. And while we are on the subject, consider the brain's own special *Time*, using millionths of our seconds. Makes yer think, mate, don't it?

Old Whitsuntides

THE DISAPPEARANCE OF Whitsuntide must astonish or sadden anybody who was young in the North when I was. In our time, Whitsuntide ranked next to Christmas. It was far more important than Easter, which came too early in the North, so that when I think of Good Fridays I only recall trying to shelter from sleet on the moors. One might almost say that it was not until about Whitsuntide that the sun came out up there. But when it did come out, we offered it something to admire, for it was on Whit Sunday that we all wore our new clothes—rather stiffly if we were self-conscious boys and youths. After I turned sixteen and went roaring out into the world, I chose my own clothes, not without colour and some wild free cuts, alarming and disgusting my father, who wore a frockcoat on Sundays and at all times was anxious not to startle the neighbours. But in my earliest teens I was still encased in sober worsteds and serges and took no pride whatever in them because they were new.

Whit Monday was the day set aside for Sunday School 'treats', as we always called them. If the chosen field were distant, we were transported there in cleaned-up coal carts, which to this hour I associate with Bradford beanfeasting.

Once there, we ran races—flat, three-legged or egg and spoon—and were given mugs of tea and large flattish buns. We lads of thirteen or fourteen let off steam and greeted the dawn of sex by chasing the girls of our own age round the outskirts of the field, which was always of a fair size. The girls giggled, screamed, and then said 'It isn't fair' when they were caught. All we did when we caught them was to let them go; we had not yet arrived then at any nymph-and-satyr business, though probably all that chasing and screaming, with so many of the girls, often quite fleet of foot, allowing themselves to be caught and shaking their curls at us as they cried that it wasn't fair, represented an archetypal sexual game. But though not without stirrings of sex, I think what chiefly appealed to us lads was the chance of letting loose our almost insane stores of energy, and doing it in an unofficial and rather disreputable fashion —and never mind the silly races, which many of us had to be bullied into running. What did not appeal to us—at least, never to me—were the dominant personalities of these organized 'treats', usually either Sunday School Super-intendents or the more active deacons. They were deter-minedly cheery and jolly with an undercurrent, soon reached, of bullying and disapproval. It is a type I heartily disliked then and have never cared for, have regarded with suspicion, ever since. Even so, these were good days, returning us exhausted, full of buns, and with the smell of early June grass still pleasantly haunting us. Incidentally, we were not allowed to wear our best new suits, with which we had gone on parade the day before.

Most of this must have vanished now, together with all traces of the Old England that worked hard but knew how to enjoy itself. Though nominally still a Christian country, we no longer celebrate the first-fruits of the spirit, as our forefathers did, but are busy demanding more money to buy the first-fruits of the Common Market at highly inflated prices. The grandsons of the lads who ran races, ate buns, and chased the girls probably spend Whit Monday wrecking telephone kiosks, smashing windows, and terrifying old women. Their fathers no longer have a holiday, to commemorate the descent of the Holy Spirit on the disciples, and this is as it should be, because they don't believe in the Holy Spirit and have nothing else to commemorate; but they will probably take the day off anyhow, just to show the weary public what is meant by 'industrial action.' And so, as people used to say, merrily we roll along.

Humour

HAVING HUMOUR MEANS continually existing in a certain atmosphere, and it has nothing to do with guffawing or giggling at jokes. All the people I have known who congratulated themselves on having 'a sense of humour', and said how important it was to have one, were several light-years away from real humour. Most stand-up comedians and their audiences are devoid of it. The funny man who is making everybody laugh in the saloon bar is no genuine humorist—unlike the quiet man in the corner who is barely smiling. Many of the most attractive men and women I have known never even pretended to have a sense of humour and detested all funny stories. And this is the next best

thing to being a genuine humorist, with a bright eye but
never a grin.

American Note

A FEW OF my staunchest friends are Americans and they
understand and appreciate my work as the very best of my
English friends do. But outside this tiny group I have
always found Americans, in various capacities and roles,
curiously undependable, fickle, warm at one time and then
suddenly cold, often quite hostile. This would happen with
American acquaintances, usually literary or theatrical, who
would change without warning, just as if, since we last met,
they had been told I had said something very unpleasant
about them, though in fact I never had. The theatrical producers in New York were less mystifying. If, during the
1930s, I arrived in New York with a play running successfully in London, the telephone would be ringing all day. If
I had just had a flop at home, there would be silence. The
publishers over there were not as bare-faced as that, but
even so, during the last twenty years, whereas I have had
the same English publisher (and for more than another
twenty before them) I must have had about half-a-dozen
different American publishers. All right: I am not an
American; I don't live and work over there; and publishing in New York is even more of a gamble than it is in
London. So there is an excuse for a lack of steadiness, for
the in-and-out game. But now we arrive at American

journalism, reviewing, and the reading public. I am quoted respectfully in one influential column and completely ignored, year after year, by twenty others. I am all 'a wonder and a wild delight' in one city, and not worth more than a review of three lines in ten other cities. Letters arrive from American readers who have just discovered my work and tell me they now don't want to read anything else, flattering but silly. The remainder of their fellow citizens— and here I mean the minority who actually read books or serious articles—if they should ever write my name, can't even spell it properly. And some of them still remember old 'anti-American' interviews with me that were in fact fabrications from beginning to end. I have received innumerable kindnesses from strangers over there and have also been roundly abused for things I never said. I have known the warmest welcomes while at the same time suffering from some of the worst professional dirty tricks I have ever encountered anywhere. Sometimes I have longed to cry, with wise old Chaucer: *O stormy peple! unsad and ever untrewe.* It can't be altogether the sheer size of the place. After all, what about those acquaintances, bewilderingly blowing hot and cold? They can't keep changing their minds just because it is three thousand miles from N.Y. to L.A.

Cambridge

IT IS RATHER odd that in the end I should have married— and very happily too—a woman who was born, brought up,

completely and brilliantly educated—in Cambridge. I say
this because during my three years there—apart from enjoying the beautiful 'backs'—I never took to Cambridge
and I don't think it ever took to me. To begin with, there
was its climate: I have been colder and hotter in Cambridge
than in any other place in England. Again, coming from
high hills I always found the Fen country depressing.
Furthermore, it wasn't on the way to anywhere, and unlike
Oxford appeared to be remote, cut off, a fortress of scholar-
ship on some remote frontier, so that, apart from the
scientists, many of its dons seemed to suffer from a frigid
conceit of themselves. Finally, though not without interest
in me once my name appeared in the London Press as well
as in the *Cambridge Review*, Cambridge society regarded
me as a North-country lout of uncertain temper. And now,
fifty-five years too late, I realize that all those people were
quite right.

A German Novel With Charm

A GERMAN NOVEL with charm. I was looking for something else, along the many shelves I have given over to
fiction, when I came upon *The Court of Fair Maidens*, the
English translation of *Hof der schönen Mädchen* by one
Wilhelm Speyer. It was published by Gollancz in 1936. It
has a lively Introduction by my lively old friend, Hendrik
Willem van Loon, a giant helping of Dutch gusto. (In my
experience, Dutchmen tend to be dull or anything but dull,

like van Loon.) I read this *Court of Fair Maidens* with pleasure, which is why it found a place on my shelves, and now, after nearly 40 years, I have read it again, I think with even more pleasure. It is a mixture of high comedy and delicious period detail, with occasional passages that have depth and insight, especially into the nature of Woman, as unexpected as the charm in a German writer. The novel is set in a small German court in the year 1805, just before and then just after the battles (which we never see) of Ulm and Austerlitz.

Perhaps I found this *Court of Fair Maidens* all the more enjoyable because it is set in this Napoleonic Age that has always fascinated me. Indeed, in the later 1920s I had made up my mind to write a tremendous novel, based on a central character and so not at all like *War and Peace*, that would divide its action between the England, France, Germany, of this period. (The hero was to have been of mixed descent.) And indeed, with this novel in mind, I had begun to acquire volumes of letters and memoirs of this Napoleonic Age. But then a fellow novelist and close friend (dead now), who was about to begin a longish novel with this Age as its background, asked to borrow some of this material. As I was turning from ambitious fiction to the Theatre, I let him borrow what he needed. A year or two later, after his novel had been published, I suggested he should now return these books. To my astonishment, he cried, 'But you *gave* them to me.' I had done nothing of the kind, and he knew it. So why did I accept, probably with a shrug, this outrageous statement? Because with him the collecting and ordered possession of books were an obsession, beyond rationality and decent friendly manners: he had to have a fine large Library. I on my part didn't share this obsession at all. I owned a lot of books—and have still more today—but never collected them. Half of them belong to a working library, enabling me to live in the country without having to rush to London to check something; and the other half feed my taste for desultory reading, often in bed. Which explains how I came to re-read and thoroughly enjoy *The Court of Fair Maidens* which, incidentally, somebody ought to put into paperback.

Problems

THERE ARE SOME readers who might welcome a dictum of mine. I am thinking now of those readers who are concerned about public affairs and keep on reading or listening to commentators, experts on politics or economics, but cannot help finding them curiously unsatisfactory, not stupid but disappointingly vague and empty, like a doctor explaining at length a disease for which he has no real diagnosis. So for their sake I shall repeat here what I have said before. A great many of our problems, so often discussed in terms of politics and economics, *are in fact psychological*. They cannot be understood without some idea of the way men's minds are working just below, of the pressures of fear or the gleams of hope that reach them from their inner worlds. And one reason why we are always finding ourselves in difficulties is that we lack, in public affairs, large-scale imaginative men who might intuitively perceive the psychological aspects of such affairs, and the persons who wrestle with them.

Woman

What is bettre than wisdom? Womman. I am again quoting Chaucer. *And what is bettre than a good womman? No-thing.* No matter how and when it came to be written, this seems to me to represent a sensible old man's opinion. When we are young men, raging with lust but at the same time magically entangled with that archetype of Woman in our unconscious, what Jung calls the *Anima*, we see girls through a mist of enchantment and don't know what they are really like. In middle-age, it is ten to one we take a cool cynical view of the sex, beyond enchantment but still not seeing women—especially good women—as they really are. It is in old age, if we have not been eaten up by vanity and self-love, that we are ready to agree with that speech of Chaucer's.

Talk to the Wife

A LESSON TO be learnt from many a Sports Page. But we will take one example. A highly-skilled football centre-forward is offered a transfer at a gigantic fee, some of which comes to him. Now here is no milksop but a very tough athlete, who must go out every Saturday to face the cheers and boos of huge crowds and the possibility that he may be carried off the field with a serious injury. Now while managers and the Press are hammering away for a decision

from him, this robust character does not immediately agree
to the transfer. And why is that? Because, he says, he must
talk to his wife and discover what she thinks about it. No
'male chauvinism' here, in this very masculine world.
Women's lib, please note.

Crime Novels

IN WHAT SHOULD properly be called 'crime novels' and
not 'detective stories', the top three for intelligent readers,
English as well as American, writers who can not only be
read but re-read, seem to be these. First, the old maestro,
Dashiell Hammett, who changed the whole style of narra-
tion itself. Secondly, Raymond Chandler, whom I knew
and liked and praised before America discovered him—
not a born storyteller but a master of memorable scenes
and witty comment. And now Ross Macdonald, with his
dogged Lew Archer following circulatory trails at all hours
of the night, a thoroughly humane and decent bloodhound.
(But perhaps rather too fond of forcing his imagery.) But
on the basis of being able to be re-read, in bed at a late
hour, I should like to add a fourth to this American trio.
This is Rex Stout, now in his later eighties. His enormously
fat detective, Nero Wolfe, who rarely leaves his house and
his orchids, is a triumph You are asked to believe that
he is an astoundingly clever man, and for once you are
convinced that he is, for he talks and behaves like one. Not
only that, but Wolfe's assistant and Stout's narrator,

the ebullient and impudent Archie Goodwin, is also a triumph. So too are their friends and acquaintances and the whole New York setting, much harder, I imagine, to maintain dramatically than the Southern California of Chandler and Ross Macdonald, at once opulent and sleazy, with crime and violence built into it. And all Stout's detail, never overdone, always seems to me convincing: I never find myself rejecting anything, as I have to do occasionally with the other three. Nor is there a lack of social content and criticism. Try, as a tasting sample, Stout's *The Doorbell Rang*, in which the F.B.I. is made to look silly—surely a brave tale to be told by an elderly popular writer. I have sworn never to set foot again in New York, not because of possible 'muggings' but because it is expensive, sour, and now offers me little I want to see and hear; but I heartily wish I could return to it, late at night in bed, with new stories of that brownstone house where Nero Wolfe growls and Archie Goodwin tries to jeer him into action before going off to dance with Lily Rowan at the Flamingo. Bravo—and greetings—to clever Rex Stout, who incidentally must be the only energetic thin man who ever created, for our admiration, a very fat man, who rarely even went as far as his front door.

Lloyd Osbourne

PROWLING AMONG MY books I plucked out the final volume of Stevenson's *Vailima Letters*, which I hadn't looked at for many years. (Probably not since 1950, when I gave the Centenary address at Edinburgh, though I had read him often enough before then.) In his last letter to Sidney Colvin, what follows leapt out at me:

> O, it is bad to grow old. For me it is practically hell. I do not like the consolations of age. I was born a young man; I have continued so; and before I end, a pantaloon, a driveller—enough again. But I don't enjoy being elderly . . .

He was then only 44, but had only a few more weeks to live, though during those weeks—as often happens—he recovered from his low spirits and was feeling lively and energetic the very day he was struck down. This is clearly conveyed by Lloyd Osbourne's account of the death and burial of R.L.S., a fine piece of prose in which we can catch an echo of Stevenson's cadences. It begins:

> He wrote hard all that morning of the last day; his half-finished book, *Hermiston*, he judged the best he had ever written, and the sense of successful effort made him buoyant and happy as nothing else could. In the afternoon the mail fell to be answered; not business correspondence—for this was left till later—but replies to the long, kindly letters of distant friends, received but two days since, and still bright in memory.
>
> At sunset he came downstairs; rallied his wife about the forebodings she could not shake off; talked of a lecturing tour to America that he was eager to make, 'as he was now so well,' and played a game at cards with her to drive away her melancholy. . . .

After reading the whole beautifully-wrought piece, I began

thinking about Lloyd Osbourne, who had shared those South Seas voyages and islands with R.L.S.—and the making of books too, adding something of his own youthful high spirits to *The Wrong Box* and *The Wrecker*. I tried several reference books but couldn't discover when and where Lloyd Osbourne died. But I certainly remember meeting him more than once in the Garrick Club—I think, in the later 1920s—and recall, though not sharply, his rather dry but courteous manner, his long face and composed features (very American) over which glints of humour came and went. What memories he must have enjoyed!—and kept so sternly to himself. He didn't belong to the 1920s at all, coming among us out of another world.

Bridie

PULLING OUT AN odd volume of Stevenson's tales and fables, I found the following written opposite the title page:

> *To J.B. Priestley D.Litt, LLD.*
> *From James Bridie, LLD., MD.,*
> *(Regius Professor of Inertia*
> *& Casual Alcoholism in the*
> *University of Skerryvore)*
> *March 1940.*

And at once there jumped into my mind, together with a pang of regret, the image and quality of my friend Osborne

Henry Mavor, who preferred to write as James Bridle—as
I shall call him here. In the 30s and 40s we were often supposed to be rivals in the Theatre, but in fact we were friends
who appreciated each other's work and stayed more than
once at each other's houses. Indeed, there was affection in
our friendship, even though we never quite understood each
other, perhaps because he was very much a Scot and I was
a sort of foreigner from across the Border. Though it was
nearly a quarter of a century ago, I recall only too well the
evening when I received the news of his death. I had been
staying with him not long before and didn't even guess there
was anything going wrong, though he did smilingly dismiss an idea for the pair of us to write plays for the 1951
Exhibition season. Early in January 1951, being 'fast with
myself' as we used to say in Yorkshire—that is, at a
bewildered loose end—I decided to revisit the ranch in
Arizona, then go down to stay at Guadalajara, Mexico, then
keep a promise to stay with Raymond Chandler in La Jolla.
I was still at the Arizona ranch when I learnt that Bridie
had died. With the news came a terrible feeling of desolation; I was 6000 miles from home and anybody who had
ever given a thought to Bridie, anybody with whom I could
share my grief and drink a glass of Scotch to his memory.
That night's desolation crept like a stain over the rest of
my journey. I drank my share of tequila in Guadalajara—
and even visited the town where it is made—but I can't
recall one happy day there.

Looking up his birthdate I was surprised to find that
Bridie was born as late as 1888, making him only six years
older than I was. I had always felt he belonged to another
generation. He was a large man in all ways, with something
always happening in that massive head of his. There were

[161]

mixed in him a doctor, an unsystematic philosopher, a man with an eye for a brilliant scene, whatever passes for an imp in Scotland, and—no pejorative sense here—an enthusiastic and combative amateur of the Theatre. (This last not a criticism of his ability, rather a suggestion of the atmosphere in which he seemed to move.) We are told that Shaw, speaking well above the snowline of his mountain of conceit, said to Bridie, 'If there had been no me there would have been no you.' And Bridie, resting on no mountain himself, seems to have accepted this. But I don't. There are scenes of his that have the brilliance and intellectual force of Shaw at his best, but they were two very different men who approached the Theatre from two very different directions. Finally, though there are plays of Bridie's—pieces as varied as *Tobias and the Angel*, *The Sleeping Clergyman*, *Mr Bolfry*—that should have a permanent place in the British Theatre, I always felt, as I never did with Shaw, that the man himself was greater than the work. There was gold in him that had never been brought out, washed and polished for the public view. And I realize now how much I have been missing him.

Not Psychic

BECAUSE I HAVE long been interested in the Time problem and, to a lesser degree, in certain forms of paranormal phenomena, I have had many letters from people who are 'psychic' and assume that I am 'psychic' too. But in fact I am not 'psychic' at all. One example will explain what I mean. For years I owned—living there for months at a time—an old house in the Isle of Wight called Billingham Manor. It was said to be haunted, and there was even a book written about it. Some visitors reported that they had seen or heard strange things. My son, then a very small boy, once declared, 'I don't like that little old woman who stares at me.' But I never saw anything, and all that I ever heard, when reading in bed late, were the various little creaks and groans of an old house settling down for the night. And while I have had many strange dreams, some of them, I believe, precognitive, I appear to be completely insensitive to all those messages and manifestations from 'behind the veil' apparently experienced by the 'psychic'. In this department at least I am one of the thickest of the thick. However, it doesn't follow that I reject all 'psychic' experiences, even though I am certainly no Spiritualist, for reasons I have given elsewhere. For example, I was in the confidence of one woman (dead now), related to me by marriage, who was undoubtedly 'psychic' as far as the living were concerned, and it was on one extraordinary experience—or, rather, series of experiences—of hers that I based a play called *The Long Mirror*, which I must confess I have largely forgotten now. What I do remember is that Jean Forbes-Robertson, who played the lead in its original production, took it on tour so often, when she had nothing better to do, that finally I told her to stop paying me any royalties on it. I doubt if anybody on the English-speaking stage could play a 'psychic' better than the gifted tragic Jean, though she herself, I feel, was no more a 'psychic' than I am. Unless of course the pair of us were 'psychics' without knowing it.

Ages

IN BOYHOOD AND early youth, I always *felt* much older than adults, friends of the family and the like, took me to be. So when they asked me what seemed to me a serious question, I answered it seriously, perhaps almost weightily, and then I saw them exchanging amused glances. I can recall an actual instance. Probably about the time I was entering my early teens, I was asked what I thought of the Bradford Amateur Operatic Society's latest production, and I replied, no doubt solemnly, 'The chorus is excellent, but some of the principals are weak.' They had asked for my opinion, and there it was, and I couldn't see why they should be so amused. Now of course the whole thing is reversed. I *feel far younger* than I appear to be. So I often give flippant answers to solemn questions, and while people may not be amused, I notice a startled glance or two coming my way. It is only in middle life that we feel the age we are, and this means there are fewer misunderstandings—but it can be a bit dull.

School Hours

THERE IS A lot of fuss now about children having their school hours cut down because of staff shortages. And quite right too, I have no doubt. But during my last three or four years at school, it would have been all the same, except I would have escaped much boredom, if my attendance had been cut down to a couple of hours a day. This is because I took so little interest in some subjects—the whole of science, for a start—that I could have been better employed elsewhere; and that with the subjects I did care about I was so far ahead that I might as well have been sent home until the rest of the class caught up with me. Why, even with only two hours, it might have been a good idea to let me spend one of them occasionally at the girls' school next door, learning how to cook.

Literary Review

THIS PROBABLY ISN'T fair, though I doubt if I am trying to be fair in these pages. But when I received this morning an appeal to support a literary Review, together with a glimpse of its contents, I found myself looking again in *On Writing and Writers*, which consists of extracts from the notebooks of Professor Walter Raleigh. In this example he was preparing a lecture on William Hazlitt, a great critic who was always ready to write about human life, books being only an excuse; and here I must add that these notes were probably written nearly seventy years ago, certainly well before the First War. And this is what he could say even then, when Eng. Lit. Departments hadn't proliferated round the world:

Criticism is not the exciting thing it was in the brave days when the critics were few and bold. It has become an industry of the workshops, carried on by those who look at new books, and look at nothing else. The greater part of critics are parasites, who, if nothing had been written, would find nothing to write. Until they meet with a live author, they cannot get to work; and they are not unwilling, in case of necessity, to infest one another. Shakespeare says what he thinks of life; Coleridge says what he thinks of Shakespeare; the modern essayist says what he thinks of Coleridge; we say what we think of the essayist—where is all this to stop? It goes on until the parasite that completes the chain is too small to nourish another. . . . .

Unfair—unfair! No doubt. But all the same I don't propose to subscribe to that literary Review.

Early Love

AFTER READING A piece on First Love (it started at 14), I went flashing down the years and arrived at about 1908. I contrived to be in love then with two very different goddesses. One was Miss Mabel Sealby, who was playing Principal Girl in the Bradford Theatre Royal pantomime; the other, my own age, was the girl next door. As I wasn't allowed to do my own theatre-going then, I saw Miss

Sealby only for one performance; I never wrote to her, never hung around the Stage Door. But her saucy black curls haunted me—she was not one of your altogether-too-demure principal girls, anaemic creatures—and every time she was mentioned in our local press then her name blazed out at me. When we were told she might be leaving the cast, after some saucy-curl dispute with the management, my city, dark enough, went into sable hangings. It was all worship at a distance, with the image of the goddess slowly fading, and oddly enough, for I think Miss Sealby had a long career and later I was always going to West End theatres, I never saw her again. On the other hand, I was always seeing the girl next door, but only through the side baywindow of our front room, where I loitered, just to catch a quick glimpse of her. The truth is, her parents and mine were not on friendly terms, and she and I never went to the same parties, so we never exchanged a word. Mine was simply a loitering-staring-dreaming relationship. Not a smile, not a look, rewarded me. My love had to exist on a meagre diet of mere glimpses of that beautiful haughty face. (If I should be asked now how a girl of 14 could have a beautiful haughty face, I would have to shake my head. But there it was —*then*.) To creep closer to her, I searched romantic poems and historical novels that offered me her name; and here she was well ahead of Miss Mabel Sealby, whose first name could not carry me very far into the realm of romance. I shall be told—there are always these types about—that my First Love, so divided, so bodiless, so silent, is a fraud, not worth an entrance into the list. Yet it is a fact that some time about 1908 I contrived to exist, while playing a great deal of football and gobbling more than one helping of suet pudding a frail poetic being, a junior

Shelley, in this high rarefied atmosphere of double enchantment, without even a kiss during Postman's Knock coming
my way.

Passing Thought

HOW HAPPY WE ought to be nowadays! Just consider if
you can manage it without vertigo, the innumerable research
scientists, experimental psychologists, psychiatrists, sociol-
ogists, who are toiling and then bringing out reports at conferences and pronouncements in the public press, all on our
behalf! Why, it makes me feel that I spent my childhood,
boyhood, youth, in the Dark Ages. Only the prejudices and
sheer stupidity of old age can account for the feeling I have
at times that we don't seem to have arrived, after so much
care and public expense, out into clear sunlight, illuminating the eager eyes of youth and the contented faces of the
old.

Maugham

NOW AND AGAIN, after shaving and wiping my face, I
have 'done a Somerset Maugham' in the mirror. To do
this I have widened my mouth, pulled down each end of it,
thrust forward the lower half of my face and tilted back

the upper half. I achieved a passable imitation of Maugham's
grimly defiant effect. Was he defying the world, his readers,
or the critics? (One of them, a big gun, Edmund Wilson,
was outrageously unfair to him—'A half-trashy novelist,
who writes badly—' for while Maugham had no gift of
style, he wrote as well as Wilson ever did. But then
Wilson was savagely prejudiced against England and most
English writers.) But then again, it is possible that Maugham's stammer had something to do with the aggressive
arrangement of his features. I met him occasionally in
London and two or three times in or near his imposing
Villa Mauresque at Cap Ferrat, and I always found him
agreeable company. (I never knew or cared what he said
about me behind my back, in one of his bitchy moods, because mine is a malicious profession—so why worry?)
I once said of him that every time he published a volume
of short stories he closed half a continent to himself,
for there can be no doubt he made too much unscrupulous
use of gossip he picked up in planters' clubs and homes out
East. Even so, his short stories, deservedly popular, probably represent his best work. He is not impressive as a
serious dramatist and his early successes were routine
Edwardian fashionable Theatre, but he had a middle vein of
sardonic comedy—e.g. *The Circle* and *Home and Beauty*—
that is excellent, and certainly the two plays above deserve
fairly constant revival. In spite of its monstrous caricature
of Hugh Walpole (and when Maugham received the same
rough treatment from a woman writer, he immediately
applied for an injunction), *Cakes and Ale* is a good novel,
far better than the more ambitious *Razor 's Edge*. It is far too
long since I read *Of Human Bondage* for me to pronounce
judgment on it, but I fancy it has been overrated, though

the futile affair with the waitress is a valuable example of Jung's 'projection of the Anima.' Where I think Maugham has been under-valued is in his travel and autobiographical notes—I have very pleasant memories of his *Gentleman in the Parlour*, never mentioned now, and in *The Summing Up* and *A Writer's Notebook* he offers us some good honest reading. It is often forgotten that Maugham, with wide cultural interests, had a well-stored mind. His chief weakness, I feel, is that he was so determined to be 'realistic' and free from illusion and humbug that all too often he ignored the hazy frontiers of personality, the gleam and shadows somewhere along the edge of the mind, the bewildering sense of another transcendent reality, the terror and beauty of our inner worlds. Though he must have been aware of all this, he depended too much on daylight and commonsense, tea and cocktails.

Women and Criticism

MOST WOMEN, ENGAGED in the same work, will ask for advice or seek instruction more readily and gratefully than most men will. On the other hand, nine women out of ten will immediately resent adverse criticism that a man would accept or shrug off. It is not that women generally behave worse than men—they don't. But in this matter of adverse criticism they suffer because their minds are rarely divided into compartments as most men's are. Instinctively they tend to run everything together, so what begins as a little bit of criticism can soon be seen as proof that the person who made it was really expressing his or her mounting all-round disapproval, deepening dislike, possible hatred. So a man who says to a woman in an edgy voice, 'You've made a mistake here', is asking for trouble. Let him smile and say, 'Very good—excellent—but perhaps a mistake has crept in here—' I am sorry to add that most of the women I know will not accept this little piece at all. 'Silly old-fashioned nonsense!' they will cry. Which I must then accept—or shrug it away.

Drolls and Childhood

WE OWE LARGE-SCALE comic characters, of the sort that endure in fiction and drama, to our childhood. If we have completely forgotten our childhood we cannot create such characters, and I doubt if we could even enjoy them. It is not that they are copies of remembered relatives and family friends; if they were they would probably be lifeless. But childhood memories supply a mixed lot of voices, faces, postures, odd habits, absurd turns of speech, and so on; and out of this material the comic characters are fashioned and brought to life. But it is a curious kind of life. We borrow the atmosphere in which they exist directly from our childhood. When we are very young we see these funny relatives and family friends as we never see people later in life. They seem to us gigantically themselves, unchanging,

immortal. So no famous comic characters have their existence in ordinary time; just as childhood doesn't exist in
ordinary time, which we have to grow up to understand.
(Falstaff never really took to his bed and died: that
was Shakespeare desperately trying to get rid of him.)
I feel sure that all the people who find such characters
tiresome wear their adulthood like armour and never return
for two minutes to their childhood. But the rest of us have
an enduring affection for these giant daft creatures partly
because they constantly restore us to another world, when
we were small and knelt on the stairs and peered between
the banisters, to see the grotesque immortals arriving.

Viennese Operettas

GLAD TO READ a piece by Neville Cardus in the *Guardian*
about Vienna, beginning with some warm praise of Lehar,
Fall, Oscar Strauss. They were the composers of the Vien-
nese operettas that were so popular in the years before the
First War. Cardus said that this music curled into his young
heart, and I can say the same. The operettas, I believe,
were very broadly adapted for the English stage—with
more business for well-known comedians—but the original
music was still there. It was very good music of its kind,
and, incidentally, it was played by orchestras that even in
the provincial tours really were orchestras and not the
theatre equivalent of an hotel dance band. Young as I was
then, and enchanted by this Central European music, I

felt there was something faintly decadent about it. Certainly it was superior to our jolly-good Edwardian musical-comedy tunes, but it came to us from a distant capital city that was rather more corrupt than ours. Its sweetness was that of fruit just before it goes rotten. I never knew that old Vienna, and indeed I paid my first visit there—the first of many visits—just after the Second War. It was then an occupied, darkened, half-starving city, but later of course everything was better, though a long way removed from the Vienna of Franz-Josef, the operettas and the stories of Schnitzler. Though I always liked being there, I felt something rather dull, rather sad, had oozed into its atmosphere. Even so, I must say that after the tragic events in Hungary in the 1950s, the aristocratic ladies I had met at parties, suddenly coming to life, helping to run the refugee camps near the Hungarian frontier, behaved like brave and compassionate good neighbours. A last thought here, with the other Vienna and its operettas still in mind—how sadly scarce now is enticing and memorable *light music*!

Powys—In Spite Of

HERE IS A book I should like to see in paperback everywhere, in place of all those sexy hot girls, secret agents, private eyes and dead blondes. It is *In Spite of* or *A Philosophy for Everyman*, published in 1953 by John Cowper Powys. It is not—and doesn't pretend to be—one of his major works, but even so it might provide a life-raft for hundreds of thousands who can't help feeling they are on sinking ships. It says we can live a satisfying and even exciting life—and now I run through the chapter headings —*In Spite of*—Experts, Loneliness, Pride, Orthodoxy and Heresy, Madness, Class, Insecurity, Belief, Other People. And Powys, a remarkable man, wasn't living one way while telling people they should try to live in quite a different way; he wasn't, so to speak, making a fortune, surrounded by admiring acquaintances, while suggesting frugality and a solitary existence. He was himself, in almost all respects, the *In Spite of* triumphant man. And readers should not hang back because the book was written over twenty years ago. Believe me, it is far more up-to-the-minute and important now than it was then. We have been hard at it piling up *In Spite ofs* for years and years. But all this doesn't mean that I agree with everything Powys says. Why should I? Wanting us to enjoy ourselves more, the old man didn't demand agreement. He wasn't in the conversion business.

Scott Fitzgerald's Theory

NOT HAVING LOOKED at it for years I was dipping into *Tender is the Night*, a disaster as a complete novel but with writing in it that makes Scott Fitzgerald a prince among his contemporaries. I had dipped towards the end, when the Diver world was coming to pieces, and the sense of exhaustion in there made me remember Fitzgerald's curious ideas of our emotional life. He thought we were all given a certain amount of emotion, like a capital sum on which we could draw freely, but that when we came to the end of it, we were emotionally bankrupt, drained out, exhausted. This was no idle fancy but a genuine belief that deeply influenced him both in his life and his work. It largely explains his desperate drinking, rather as if there might have been some small sums of emotion he had overlooked and more gin might help him to find them. Here he trapped himself. A loss of energy could account for a loss of feeling. And the huge haunting negative thought itself could be using up energy, quite apart from daft drinking bouts and all the hangovers. I am not suggesting that our capacity for deep feeling remains unchanged. When we begin ageing fast—as I am sure I am doing—our emotional life loses both breadth and depth. We don't really *feel* as much as we used to do, probably because the energy is no longer adequate. But of course Fitzgerald had hardly reached middle-age when he died, though physically he was older than his years. But while I realize all manner of circumstances conspired against him, I can't help suspecting that he was partly the victim of a wrong idea. He had been busy for too long emotionally bankrupting himself.

A Pessimist?

WRITING YESTERDAY TO a colleague about an ambitious theatrical enterprise, for which I have no direct responsibility and take only a tiny royalty, I used a phrase or two that my wife said would add nothing to his confidence and enthusiasm. She didn't say, 'That's just like you!' because—thank Heaven!—she avoids that style of reproach; but no doubt she has often thought it. The truth is that at heart I am—and have long been—a pessimist. I like to think that I disguise this very well, being reasonably cheerful in company—and at one time fond of clowning. But possibly this is an illusion. (The preposterous label, *Jolly Jack*, was first used ironically.) Certainly I am not one who looks instinctively on the bright side. Few clouds of mine have a silver lining. Mark Tapley is one of my non-favourite Dickens characters: I would have found him unendurable. One home of gassy optimism is the Theatre, and this explains the astonishing amount of rubbish to be found in it. It also explains why I have never been a really good Theatre man, in spite of bringing a fair amount of expertise to it, for I generate little or none of that enthusiasm which is its oxygen. Again, the spirits of most people rise when they are about to go on a long and perhaps romantic journey; but what I usually feel is a vague foreboding—not wondering if the plane will crash, the ship sink, but darkly dubious about the whole troublesome and expensive jaunt. I am pessimistic too about larger questions, holding that all talk of almost automatic progress is claptrap, and that either we go from bad to worse or—at best—what will be gained from the swings will have been lost on the roundabouts. It is true that now and again a temporary optimism can overlay my natural pessimism, as it did in the Second War. But from this I return to watch the scene darkening again. Why should this be when I don't lack energy or a natural immediate ebullience? I can hazard only one guess. In my later teens, as I have described elsewhere, all was well: the days were bright with expectation. But then came the First War and a long term in the Army, years divided between the murderous, the tedious and the idiotic. Then three years at Cambridge, where I never felt at home. Then an appalling domestic tragedy, working overtime with despair at my elbow. So probably the roots of being began to harden and darken. This had one result that people may have noted. In my creative work I tended to be a happy-ending man. This was not a bid for popularity. (Unhappy-enders have on the whole done better than I have.) The point is, that in the tiny worlds I created myself I tried to defy my pessimism. All would come right here, if nowhere else. But as a few persons with insight have observed—no matter how lively and hopeful the scene, somewhere behind it, occasionally showing through, is the shadow of a certain melancholy and more than a suggestion of pessimism, that pessimism I am not holding up for admiration but am trying to explain.

Old Phoney?

AS A SOUVENIR of that Freedom of the City affair in Bradford, the Town Clerk kindly sent me a coloured photograph of myself, abut 12″ by 14″ and handsomely mounted. I am gazing benevolently out of it, holding a pipe in one hand and in the other a picture, one of my own, presented to the

City Council. Everybody living in or visiting this house warmly admired this photograph, and so did I for a time. But then the oftener I glanced at it the more I began to entertain certain doubts, spiced with self-derision. And now I am sure I am looking at the portrait of a complacent old phoney—*NOT ME*!

Happiness and Admass

HOW TO EXPLAIN the trouble we are in almost all the time now? I suggest we might turn from politics and economics, if only as a change from wearisome commenting, to psychology. On this level I venture an explanation. But I exclude from it really poor people (offering us an urgent task), who dream about a few square meals, shoes with no holes in them, roofs that don't leak. The rest of us feel we have a right to be happy, an idea never accepted by our great-grandfathers, often far happier than we ever are. But happiness as a target or the entrance to a fabled land is a mirage, being by its very nature the by-product of a good way of living, a psychological bonus. But we have been told over and over again—this repetition is an essential part of *Admass*—that not only have we a right to be happy but that happiness will arrive as soon as we have more money and begin to spend it. (This applies to all classes except the super-rich—and I have met a few of them—whose only chance of escaping satiety and miserable sus-

picion is through giving away most of their money.) But
the catch here is that when we have arrived at Square Three,
and don't feel happy and not even reasonably contented, we
begin to believe that what will do the trick is Square Four,
where there is more money. And so it goes on, with the
golden gleam receding. Meanwhile, the sure psychological
foundation is cracking badly and indeed has great holes in it.
Let us look at this from two different sides. Years ago a
man made shoes, took a pride in his shoes, and because they
were good shoes his business rapidly expanded. His son,
who inherited the business, was less interested in shoes and
more interested in the money to be made out of them. His
grandson, our contemporary, now head of a very large
concern, thought first about profit and saw shoes as a pro-
duct, just good enough to pass muster, that would bring
in the profit. Something nourishing had gone out of that
family: grandfather had the best chance of happiness. Now
we take a workman of that same generation. Probably he
was over-worked and underpaid; and I hope we agree that
this was not good enough. Even so let us assume—and it
happened often—that he was a skilled man who took a pride
in his work, just as grandfather did in his shoes. There was
something here for him to stand on, to increase his self-
respect, to offer him some contentment at the day's end.
Psychologically he would be far better off than any grandsons of his now fretting, grumbling, shouting to get out of
Square Three into Square Four, where the money was
really rolling in, and happiness was just round the corner,
where you might be able to forget you were responsible
for some sloppy workmanship. And this is not an attack
on employers and employees: it is part of a plea for a little
more psychological insight.

The Rubbish Gets Through

A SMALL POINT but not to be despised, worth a sentence or two. Whenever a fault develops in our postal services, over and over again the same thing happens to me. Letters of some importance, together with letters eagerly awaited from friends, fail to be delivered. But all the stuff I don't want, silly letters, bills, advertisments, seem to come through without a hitch. Now why should this always happen? I suspect that the postal sorting departments are taken over by that Malicious Iron Power, which rarely misses a chance of this sort to prove that it still exists and is hard at work, even if the G.P.O. isn't.

Always Bach

OVER AND OVER again I have noticed that educated people, who don't really care for music, when asked about it say they can't spare much time for listening but that when they do—it must be Bach. How refreshing it would be to meet a pair of these people who declared without hesitation that for them it must be Tchaikowsky! And why don't people realize that the most effective and heart-warming answer to any cultural question is the exact truth? Boswell once found Dr Johnson reading a history of Birmingham and ventured to say he thought it might be rather dull. The great man said it was very dull indeed.

Nihilistic Criticism

FOR SOME YEARS now, novelists, playwrights, film directors with a very bleak or dark outlook, men offering
us nihilism and pessimism, have been consistently over-
praised by many of the younger critics. What is talent is
hailed as genius. Now why is this? I think it is because the
critics themselves are equally nihilistic, pessimistic, des-
pairing, but are afraid of declaring this, telling us directly
how hopeless they feel, so they insist upon over-estimating
and over-praising any novelist, playwright, film director,
who does the dismal job for them. They are busy life-
denying by proxy.

No Tax Haven

CERTAINLY I GRUMBLE about all the money I have to
pay—and have paid down the years—in income tax and
sur-tax. And I resent the fact that, after handing over a
fortune to the state, I have never had a single *Thank you*
from anybody representing it. This taxation exists in a
strange punitive atmosphere, as if we had done wrong by
working hard. Even so, I don't envy my colleagues—and
there are now a great many of them—who live abroad to
escape the tax men. It seems to me they have given the
tax men far more than I have. They have allowed these

fellows to decide where they shall live. To be rich, escaping tax, is not very important, it seems to me, whereas I feel it is very important to live where I want to live—in England.

The Energy We Had

THE ENERGY WE had as schoolboys was prodigious. I am thinking now of the years 1904–1910. My friends and I walked eight miles a day simply to and from school. And often we didn't even walk, we ran around the carless streets, kicking a little ball between us, dribbling perhaps or chasing it down side-streets, rather like so many eager dogs running round and round on a walk. During holidays we played football on a neighbouring field from the middle of the morning until dusk. These were not matches between teams. Sides were roughly picked early on, and the game never stopped. Lads rushed home for dinner at various times, and then rushed back, after two or three helpings of suet pudding. The sides might dwindle to six or so or go to sixteen, which encouraged some rather rough stuff. Not until the light was going or the lad who had provided the ball—a real football this time—firmly took it home did we stop, and I might add that the field of our choice was anything but level. And that is not all. Occasionally during a holiday or on a Saturday I would go for a walk into the country with my father, who was something of a botanist (he had many interests) and would go far afield looking for some unusual wild flower; and he would walk and walk and walk, at a stiff pace if he had a destination in mind, and I would keep at his side for miles and miles and miles. Our energy, I repeat, was prodigious. And how did we keep going? The answer is simple. Our diet was crammed with starch—now regarded as the enemy. To keep down my weight, liable to go up if I merely hear a couple of sausages sizzling in the pan, I must pretend now that starch hardly exists. So where does the energy come from, the energy I need to do any work at all? From will power, madam, or such scrag ends of it as are left to me. But—oh for starch and those helpings of pud and all those daylong games of football!

American Explaining

THE REASON WHY so many American middle-aged or elderly men are extremely boring is very simple. They insist upon explaining everything, leaving nothing out, very slowly in a disastrously monotonous tone. So long before they have finished, we are tired of the subject. And so too are most of their wives, daughters, sisters, and probably even their aunts. But if these women have so much power, if America is a matriarchy, why are the tedious males allowed to go on droning away? The answer, as I have pointed out before, is that America is not a matriarchy but as a society is dominated by the male principle, to which the strategy and tactics of business, the failure or triumph of automobiles, the ingenuity of gadgets, are all immensely important, so that explanations of these matters, no matter how long and boring, must not be cut short.

A Warning

WHEN PEOPLE TELL me that I am looking very well—and this is always happening—I don't feel pleased but irritable. What nonsense they talk! What do they know about it? One of these days, I tell myself darkly, I'll be slapped on the back and fall down dead.

For Some Young Men

THIS IS WHERE the trap is waiting, my lads. So long as you are healthy, get enough to eat and drink, and keep out of the dock, it hardly matters what you do in your twenties. But you can't stay in your twenties, and the men who try to soon become embarrassing. So give a thought now and again to yourselves at forty-five, because what is happening to you then may make the difference between a life and half a life, most of it sour.

Too Impatient

DURING THE 1930s and 40s a lot of illwill came my way. My friends said this was envy, but I think it was largely my own doing. Almost always I was driving myself too hard, pursuing two or three different careers at the same time. I was never really arrogant—arrogance is not one of my failings—but may have appeared to be, simply because I was extremely impatient. It was easy for me to concentrate entirely upon any matter in hand, then to work quickly. If other people would not—or could not—do this, I was probably brusque with them, possibly sounding more intolerant and contemptuous than I really felt. I was not trying to lord it over them because I was better-known or earned more money; status and prestige never came into it; I simply felt they were not giving everything to the job, whatever it was, when I was working flat out. There were certain dimmish types in the press, the BBC, and on the fringes of theatrical production, that always made me feel particularly impatient, ready to write them off. Ralph Richardson, with whom I often worked and talked during those years, once said, 'You're too annoyed by chaps who are just trying to earn a living.' He was quite right. I hope I am not flattering myself if I add here that it was the people who saw me briefly who went around saying I was a dreadful fellow. The people who really worked with me—in the Theatre for example—nearly always wanted to join me again, and I was told many times that, contrary to all vague reports, I was remarkably easy to work with. Now I think I have lost that brusque impatient manner, that contempt for chaps who are just trying to earn a living.

Unfortunately, I have also lost the capacity for working at high pressure. I am slithering into the character of a fairly amiable and rather lazy old gent.

Coleridge Wrong

The man's desire is for the woman; but the woman's desire is rarely other than for the desire of the man. This—or something like it—has often been repeated since Coleridge first wrote it in 1827. It would not be widely accepted now, and it wasn't true even for 1827. (However, I agree that Coleridge's 'rarely' can be stretched.) Sexually experienced women can usually feel at least as much desire as men. And indeed the old tradition, spread wide and enduring through many an age, held that Woman by and large wanted a great deal more sex than men did. (There is an amusing and surprising piece by Mark Twain on this subject, though it emphasized feminine capacity rather than rapacity.) Our male ancestors deplored their wives' and mistresses' ruthless and almost insatiable desire for sex, demanding it when their partners began to be fearful of this tax on their virility. It was one of the burdens beginning to exhaust and age a man. (The candid Wife of Bath asked for a supply of *young husbands.*) Probably cynics and comic writers made too much of this theme, but I fancy it is much closer to the truth than Coleridge's *woman's desire is rarely other than for the desire of the man.* And after all

how much intimate knowledge of women did Coleridge
ever acquire?

As Russian Landowner

AMONG PEOPLE WHO don't really know me I have passed
for years as an exceptionally energetic and purposeful fellow. But I know now that if I were a landowner I would
be almost exactly like so many of the Russian aristocrats
in Russian literature. Because I would shrink from making
decisions and immediately acting upon them, my estate
would be drifting towards desolation and ruin. Every
morning, catching sight of roofless barns, broken fences and
untilled fields, I would declare that something must be done
soon and would then turn my attention to the planets, the
state of literature, foreign affairs, a new way of cooking
sturgeon, and the rumour that our friend Count N. has
quarrelled with his mistress.

Catholic Converts

WITH BORN CATHOLICS I find I can jog along comfortably,
but I am usually less at ease with Catholic converts, especially

if they are fellow writers. (There was much conversion in London between the wars.) A simple soul, I fail to understand those writers who made a fuss about their conversion, brought the Catholic faith and viewpoint into their work, and yet soon turned out to be bad Catholics, rarely attending Mass, avoiding the confessional, and deliberately forcing a quarrel on their Church in public. In my simplicity, I can't help feeling that if I had undergone conversion, if at last I had *joined*, I would have wanted to be one of the pious, obeying all the rules, and not just a chap bringing a distant glare of hellfire into my fiction. Again, if I had been converted I would not be indignant if Rome did what it said it would do. Which reminds me of a morning many years ago when Alfred Noyes, a convert and a neighbour of mine then in the Isle of Wight, came in to see me. He had brought out a biggish book about Voltaire, attempting to prove that the sardonic old man was really a sincere Christian at heart; and he burst into my house breathless and shaking with fury, to gasp that Rome had placed his book on the *Index*. I said I was sorry but refused to work up any indignation. After all, I hadn't converted him. He ought to have hurried to Farm Street.

Irritating Book

IN SEARCH OF something I had written over thirty years

ago, I have just gone rapidly through a whole book, hoping
to find the passage there. Now this was a book that had
seemed to me pretty good when I had finished writing it.
Moreover, it had been highly praised by reviewers and
readers, and to this day I occasionally get letters telling
me how good it was—and is. Yet looking through it again,
after all these years, I found I could not enjoy any of it.
Somehow it seemed to me a damnably *irritating* book. At
last I could understand the people who didn't like me. As
far as that book is concerned, I don't like me.

Memory Box

WHEN THE OCCASION demands it, we can open little
memory-boxes in our minds that are closed to us in the
ordinary way. For example, when I gave the Centenary
Lecture on Arnold Bennett at Stoke, not only was I addressing a packed audience in the Town Hall (or whatever it
was) but at the same time I was doing a live broadcast for
the B.B.C.; and yet I had no script, not even a few notes to
hand, nothing to help me but my memory—for names,
books, dates and so forth. But when I am talking at ease to
one or two other people I am reduced to saying *What's-his-
name* and *Thingummy-jig* and *Where-is-it* and *I'll-forget-my-
own-name-next*: obviously a man with a bad memory. I
depend on the challenge of the occasion to open the box

for me. And, thinking it over now, I realize I will chance
this once too often.

Danger of Versatility

IN WHAT FOLLOWS, I am being quite serious. We must
suppose that instead of writing over thirty plays, together
with scores of books, I had written only eight plays—let
us say, *Dangerous Corner, Eden End, Time and the Conways,
I Have Been Here Before, When We Are Married, Johnson
Over Jordan, An Inspector Calls,* and *The Linden Tree.* (And
many of the others were quite successful.) Then we must
also suppose that instead of turning away from the Theatre,
having many other interests, I had worked hard at being a
Theatre man, I had attended every important London first
night, I had spent most of my time with Theatre people, I
missed no opportunity of presenting myself to the public, at
home and abroad, as a dramatist and had intervened as often
as possible in any discussion of the Theatre. Assuming all that,
it is my belief that on the basis of these eight plays alone I
would be enjoying a greater esteem, again both at home
and abroad, than I do now. There are two main reasons for
this. The first is that the Theatre, a feminine creature, is
suspicious of men who don't entirely give themselves to
her. The second is that in this age—unlike most others—
versatility does not enlarge a writer's reputation but re-
duces it. I might add a third reason, that in this age it pays
a man to beat his big drum as hard as he can. And I am not

denying his dramatic genius if I say that no writer understood this better than George Bernard Shaw, who could make
any publicity agent look like the chairman of a secret society.

Dead Comrade

A LETTER THIS morning from a woman in Australia, a
contemporary of mine who lived in Bradford when I did,
before the First War. She had enjoyed so many of my books
and plays etc. etc. but the real point of the letter was concerned with her brother, Irvine, whom she remembered
'speaking so often' about me because I was a friend of his
and he 'admired' me. This I doubt, though it is true he was
among my closer friends in B Company, 10th Duke of
Wellington's. He was in fact an exceptionally fine fellow,
and like many other exceptionally fine fellows he was
killed before 1916 was out. Although I had forgotten his
name, now all day I have been catching glimpses of his
face as I saw it for the last time. He had been further along
the trench where a shell had scored a direct hit. When I
spoke to him, before he was taken away, he knew he was
done for, although, like so many men desperately wounded,
he felt no pain. And his face, drained of blood but with the
ghost of a rueful grin on it, has come floating up out of the
dark river of years. His sister, now in her middle seventies,
writes because she remembers, as women always seem to
do; and now I am remembering—and perhaps the *anima
mundi* will remember us all.

Two Kinds of Malice

WHEN WE TALK about malice we ought to make a sharp distinction between light malice and heavy malice. It is unpleasant to keep company with heavy malice, when people are spitting poison and the atmosphere of the room is thick with illwill. Envy or jealousy or all-round hatred is always hard at work in heavy malice. Even a little of it goes too far. But it seems to me that light malice is entirely different, coming from another direction. It plays with the weaknesses or little absurdities of people we know and may greatly like, even love. It turns them for the time being, while one amusing reminiscence follows another, into comic characters, which we all are and should be, even to ourselves. I would be disappointed and downcast if I were solemnly assured that my friends and neighbourly acquaintances didn't discuss me and laugh—as we were doing last night about somebody else whom we like and admire—all in light malice. And easy friendly talk without any touches of light malice is like a savoury dish denied both salt and pepper.

Utopias

ONE OF THE brief notes on plays I shall never write set its scene at a frontier post. Two different groups met there:

one was trying to get into Utopia, the other was trying to get out. If I had ever written the play I would have balanced my sympathy between the two groups, but I can't help feeling that I would have been one who wanted to get out. All visits to Utopias tend to depress me. Everything that has to be done in them has already been done, long before my arrival. We are asked to enjoy them and not help to make them. But I would rather be a maker than an enjoyer. Creation reaches a deeper level of our being. I have never envied those people, who usually have a substantial private income, who contrive to turn their small private worlds into Utopias by elaborately cultivating their appreciation of 'the finer things', from music and painting to wine and food, and then go about tasting here, tasting there, well away from the rough-and-tumble of making. How much better, it seems to me, to do what one can to bring a tiny corner of the huge brutal world at least just a shade nearer to a Utopia, than to go gaping and marvelling at a country or a city that had been brought to perfection long ago, to settle for endless appreciative tasting. To put it bluntly— it is the chaps who worked at it long ago who had the fun— the fun on the surface and the deeper joy below.

The Researchers

ABOUT HALFWAY THROUGH a book, sent by an American publisher, about the Brain and its wonders, I begin to be darkly suspicious. It describes scores of experiments conducted by research teams. Some of these are innocent enough, but in others—well, sparrows are blinded, mice are given cancerous injections, rats are so manipulated that they begin to fight cats, while cats in their turn, together with dogs, become victims of the brain-surgeon's knife or the experimental electrodes. Now if this came out of a desperate desire to save human life, all might be well, but behind so many of these experiments there is merely so much scientific curiosity, material for a paper at the next conference. And it is the obvious lack in these quarters of a decent natural piety, an instinctive feeling for other living creatures, that makes me darkly suspicious. What they were doing last year to sparrows and mice, rats and cats, they may be doing in a few years' time to us fellow human beings. Not of course to chairmen of the Board, managing directors, important executives, but to mere riffraff—rebels, radicals, lazy though cheerful drunks—probably old authors.

Business Men and Artists

WE ALL KNOW about the vanity, conceit, egoism, of writers, artists, actors. But how many weary times have I heard rather stupid business men say to me, with infinite condescension, 'Oh, I read that book of yours'? Behind that kind of remark and that sort of tone are heights, depths, thicknesses of vanity, conceit, egoism, beyond the reach of writers, artists, actors.

Another Try

A SPEECH BY Vershinin in *The Three Sisters* begins: 'I often say to myself: suppose one could start one's life over again, but this time with full knowledge? Suppose one could live one's life as one writes a school composition, once in rough draft, and then live it again in the fair copy?' Long before I knew *The Three Sisters* or had read Ouspensky's *New Model of the Universe*, I was haunted by this idea, even though I have experienced the *déjà vu* effect less often than many other people seem to have done.

Life and Death

TO LIVE WITH death is also to live with life. To banish all thought of death is to begin losing the flavour, zest and quality of life. Ancient peoples—like the Egyptians, with their skeleton at the feast—understood this. Shakespeare, who knew so much, understood it too, as many a familiar quotation testifies. But now far too many people are refusing to understand it. They drive the thought and prospect of death down into the unconscious, where in the dark depths, away from the light of consciousness, death swarms and proliferates in a sinister magical existence, haunting dreams and unguarded moments of the conscious mind. In it there are now too many doors that must not be opened, too many shadowy corners left unvisited. There begins to be a loss of that vital energy which flavour, zest, quality in living, all demand. We hear of rich men, hoping to refrigerate themselves out of dying, who want to go on and on and on living when they may never have really lived at all. Our doctors used to strive to keep us reasonably healthy and still possessing some dignity. Beyond that, death was welcome. But some of them now, so determined not to offer death a victory, would cheerfully turn a patient into a whimpering mummy or a defecating vegetable. Perhaps the Mid-Victorians, for ever attending or describing death-beds and visiting graveyards, overdid it. But it is worth remembering that these same people were also more energetic and much livelier than we are. So I say again that to try to banish all thought of death, as our age attempts to do, is to begin losing the flavour, zest and quality of life.

Envoi

IF YOU HAVE arrived at this page by skipping, then what follows is not for you. But if you have not missed a piece and have been a patient reader, then let me add that I wish I had been as patient a writer. However, within the limitations of my temperament—and there are one or two pieces here on *that* subject—I have tried to do my best for over half a century, often keeping my impatience quiet by turning from one form of writing to another, quite different. We have to do what we can with ourselves, rather like a man who has inherited a circus. And after all the circus might make some good friends.